Building Violence

Building Violence

How
America's
Rush to
Incarcerate
Creates
More
Violence

John P. May
Editor

Khalid R. Pitts
Associate Editor

Sage Publications, Inc.
International Educational and Professional Publisher
Thousand Oaks ■ London ■ New Delhi

For information:

Sage Publications, Inc.
2455 Teller Road
Thousand Oaks, California 91320
E-mail: order@sagepub.com

Sage Publications Ltd.
6 Bonhill Street
London EC2A 4PU
United Kingdom

Sage Publications India Pvt. Ltd.
M-32 Market
Greater Kailash I
New Delhi 110 048 India

Printed in the United States of America

Library of Congress Cataloging-in-Publication Data

Main entry under title:

Building violence: How America's rush to incarcerate creates more
violence / edited by John P. May.
    p. cm.
  ISBN 0-7619-1459-5 (cloth: acid-free paper)
  ISBN 0-7619-1460-9 (pbk.: acid-free paper)
  1. Prisoners—Rehabilitation—United States.
2. Imprisonment—United States. 3. Violence—United States.
4. Prisoners—United States—Social conditions. 5. Prison psychology.
6. Recidivism—United States. I. May, John P.
  HV9304.B85 2000
  364.3—dc21   99-6730

This book is printed on acid-free paper.

00 01 02 03 04 10 9 8 7 6 5 4 3 2 1

Acquiring Editor:	Kassie Gavrilis
Editorial Assistant:	Anna Howland
Production Editor:	Denise Santoyo
Editorial Assistant:	Nevair Kabakian
Designer/Typesetter:	Janelle LeMaster

To Debby for your support, inspiration,
and commitment to a better world

And in memory of victims of violence including
Demonae, Dewayne, Jermaine, Albert, Lemont, Terrance,
and Rueben—nonviolent offenders who each died violently
shortly after being released from their incarceration

Contents

Part II: IMPURE JUSTICE 39

Part III: CASUALTIES OF MASS INCARCERATION 69

Part IV: THE CRUCIBLE OF VIOLENCE 111

List of Photographs

Acknowledgments

Editors May and Pitts appreciate and would like to acknowledge the contributions of the following individuals and organizations: Dr. Armond Start, Brian Prunty, L. Anthony Groves, Cynthia Randolph, Michael Robbins, Diane L. Gross, Nancy Mahon, Dr. Gloria Pitts, Estelle Hunter, Dr. Robert B. Griefinger, Ineke Haen Marshall, Deborah Leff, Mary McClymont, Craig Underwood, Ronald Harris, Nancy Reed, Rebecca Block, the Homicide Research Working Group, Cermak Health Services of Cook County, Central Detention Facility of Washington, D.C., and Prison Health Services, Inc.

Introduction

John P. May

"Hey doc, you've got to help me with this cold." As a doctor in a crowded jail, I had heard this type of complaint often. But this inmate, a man not more than 23 years old, continued by saying, "My nose is so stuffed up I can't smell nothin'. I couldn't even smell a dead body if it was in front of me." I looked at him and felt totally helpless. He might as well have had an incurable malignancy. Although I could easily remedy his nasal congestion, I knew of no cure for the despair represented in his "dead body" imagery. Then I asked, "Did you hear what you said? Why couldn't you say, 'I couldn't even smell a beautiful flower?'" Now it was his turn to feel helpless. He hesitated, and then said softly, "I guess this place is getting to me."

I understand what he meant. Every day in the jail brings another story of assault, brutality, or death. After being immersed in jail or prison, it becomes difficult to believe that the world can be anything else. Over the years, practicing medicine in the midst of this violent environment and seeing some of the same people come in and out over and over again, I have become concerned that the negative influences of prison might ultimately be expressed in society.

The chapters in this book were written by experts and practitioners who also spend a lot of time inside or studying prisons, and have come to share this concern. Could it be that the very thing we are trying to protect against—violence—is made worse as we incarcerate more people? This would be very ironic, indeed. But the question is very serious, and its answer critical, because prison systems are expanding, gaining political and economic momentum, and becoming an unmistakable part of the American landscape.

The United States is conducting a social experiment unparalleled in its size and implications. One of every eleven adult men will spend time in a state or federal prison. The financial costs seem nearly irrelevant to those who, understandably, want to feel safe but mistakenly rely on incarceration as a solution. Incarceration can be counterproductive. Although criminological research has found prisons to be useful in protecting society from some offenders, it has also found that prison reinforces criminal behavior in others. Criminological research has not been able to demonstrate convincingly that the incarceration of more people, and longer sentences, ultimately provide more security. Considering that the prison population has expanded fourfold since 1980, the certain but marginal benefit of incapacitating the few violent offenders might be offset by the damage caused by processing millions of others through the same system.

Curiously, even though evidence has shown certain prevention programs to be less costly and more effective than incarceration in making a safer society, new prison construction and tougher sentences garner more political support. The tremendous growth of the prison system should shame those who seek cost-effective solutions, but expanding incarceration apparently generates other political payoffs. The public's frustration with violence appears to be satisfied only by the vengeance that incarceration provides. The public wants not only to incarcerate, but also to punish, the wrongdoer.

From a public health perspective, however, it is provocative to consider what happens when such large portions of the population are exposed to prison influences. A diffusion of violent behavior is predictable. Prisons are toxic environments, and often affect people negatively. A young person who goes through a prison term is likely to have many further incarcerations. In some urban jails, upwards of 80% of admissions are people who have been previously incarcerated. Obviously, something is wrong when people keep returning.

Of particular concern are nonviolent offenders, the majority of persons sent to prison; they share the prison environment with violent offenders. Fewer than one third of those sent to prison have been convicted of violent offenses (murder, rape, assault, or robbery). State wardens surveyed believed that 50% of their inmates could be released into society without posing any risk. Most wardens can quickly identify the inmates who need to remain separate from free society, as well as from the rest of their incarcerated population. These are the people for whom prison was intended.

For many, social services or medical centers could provide more effective treatment than jails or prisons. People often enter the system because they created a disturbance on the streets while intoxicated, homeless, or mentally ill. In most systems, they simply do their time and return to the streets with little intervention. On a typical day, the jail staff processes dozens or even hundreds of new arrestees, including belligerent and trembling alcoholics, intravenous drug users with foul smelling abscesses, heroin users vomiting from withdrawal, decompensated mentally ill persons, and pregnant women coming down from drug highs. Most of these arrestees do not have the means or the resources to find assistance on the streets. Nearly 20% to 30% of new arrestees also have medical problems such as diabetes, hypertension, seizures, or HIV, which have been neglected or not recognized, and require complicated and expensive attention.

Although jails and prisons are termed "correctional facilities," this is truly a misnomer. There is little in the modern system of incarceration that is rehabilitative or corrective, apart from possibly interrupting some self-destructive behaviors on the streets. Rehabilitation is seldom a priority in massive prison expansion. "Maintain safety and prevent escapes" are the words that many prison wardens use to describe the extent of their mission.

Although Americans might expect programs and rehabilitation in prison, they also resent anything that could be considered beneficial for criminals. Consequently, restrictions are placed on what prisoners do and what programs exist. But without many programs or incentives for good behavior, prison officials struggle to keep control inside their increasingly crowded facilities. They often resort to isolation, power, manipulation, and force to keep the prison orderly. Inmates soon adopt these same tools.

Without rehabilitation, incarceration, like welfare, can foster dependency. For some, incarceration becomes a way of life—even a generational phenomenon. Many inmates have parents or other relatives who have been through the system. It is easy to see how this cycle develops. Young people enter the criminal justice system at the most critical time in their development toward becoming responsible and productive citizens or family providers. Whatever progress they had made toward independence and adulthood is lost. The young man or woman might have just started a new school, job, relationship, living arrangement, or parenthood. Incarceration separates them from all of this. They lose the chance to continue their education, to find or sustain meaningful employment, to seek or achieve fulfilling relationships, to nurture their children, to define themselves as capable, worthy, and respected individuals.

As they leave prison, they are several steps behind. The prison experience has created new barriers to almost every opportunity. Few employers, for example, open their doors to former prisoners. Some have so much difficulty reintegrating into society that return to prison is inevitable. The criminal justice system becomes their only source of social support, structure, discipline, validation, and even power and respect.

For some, incarceration is neither a deterrent nor a shameful experience. The threat of incarceration is much more meaningful, for example, to an employed and connected person than to one who is unemployed and disconnected. For some inmates, surviving the shame and degradation of the incarceration process simply raises their status among their peers and gives them self-esteem. I recall walking along a busy downtown sidewalk one day when a middle-aged man shouted loudly and proudly for friends and strangers to hear, "Hey doc, remember me? You took care of me when I was locked up!"

In the end, we would like a safer community. As a physician who has treated the bleeding of gunshot wounds, stabbings, and other intentional injuries, I have seen too much pain suffered by too many. Violence impacts the health and security of individuals and the community in the most devastating way. As we search for explanations of this violence, we would be remiss, I have come to learn, if we do not look carefully at our prison systems.

The purpose of this book is to look at what is happening to our society as a consequence of what is happening inside our jails and prisons. Although this book does not propose or evaluate alternatives to incarceration in detail, many good resources and studies have already done this and should be explored. In many cases, there are far more effective methods for changing behavior than imprisonment; prison and punishment are for those who deserve it. The importance of this book, then, is the caution it raises, through many varied and experienced voices, about the consequences of processing millions of our young men and women through the criminal justice system. Ignoring this caution might inadvertently raise the risk of violent events.

Part I

The Search for Security

Faced with perceptions of random violence and escalating crime in the 1980s, the United States launched a massive buildup of prison capacity. In retrospect, crime rates were not much different from cycles in other eras, but the response was a dramatic increase in incarceration, wildly disproportionate to the crime trends. The increased prison population, along with mandates for tougher conditions, has changed corrections for the 21st century. In the chapters that follow, researchers and practitioners discuss the effects and consequences on crime and prisons, and what a large prison population means to the community.

The Connection Between Crime and Incarceration[1]

Alfred Blumstein

The Crime-Punishment Conundrum

Crime and punishment have captured considerable public attention in recent years. An examination of the trends of crime and the trends of punishment over time raises some important questions about our state of knowledge in controlling crime through the criminal justice system, and about our ability to do so.

The interaction between crime and punishment is certainly a complex one. In simple terms, one might anticipate that, if crime rates increase, there should be a corresponding increase in prison populations, perhaps with a lag of a year or two to account for the processing of the most serious of the arrested offenders into prison. On the other hand, if punishment levels increase, crime-control theory suggests that deterrence and incapacitation should be reflected in a corresponding reduction in crime rates.

The relationship between these two phenomena in the United States from the 1970s to the 1990s provides an opportunity to explore how well our current theory can account for the trends. Even though incarceration rates increased steadily and are now almost quadruple what they were twenty years ago, most crime rates have remained confined within a fairly narrow range, with no strong trend. Perhaps most strikingly, we have not seen the anticipated downward trend in crime rates that might have been anticipated as a result of the growth in incarceration. This poses a conundrum that has not yet been adequately examined.

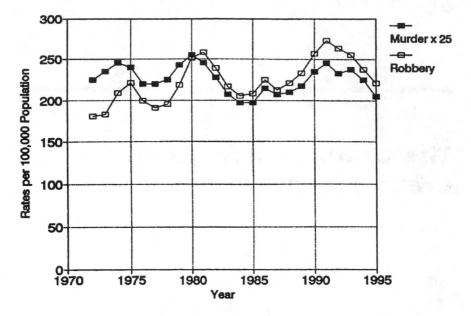

Figure 1.1   UCR rates of murder and robbery.

SOURCE: Blumstein, A. (1988). U.S. criminal justice conundrum: Rising prison populations and stable crime rates. *Crime and Delinquency, 44*(1), 127-135.

Trends in Crime Rates

In the United States over the past 20 years, crime rates have fluctuated, but remain near a fairly stable mean. Figure 1.1 displays the reported rates of murder and robbery in the United States (with murder scaled up by a factor of 25 to put it on the same scale as robbery). These data are based on reports of crime by the public to the police, and by police to the FBI's Uniform Crime Reports (UCR).

Figure 1.1 shows clearly that the reported rates for these two most serious crimes have been fairly stable, ranging between 200 and 250 persons per 100,000 for robbery and between 8 and 10 persons per 100,000 for murder. The slope of the trend line for the murder series is not significantly different from zero, and is slightly upward for robbery—an annual trend of less than 1.4% of the mean rate for robbery. The fluctuations in the two rates track each other fairly closely, reaching peaks and troughs at about the same time.

This stability or relative lack of trend in crime rates is certainly at marked variance with the general view of the American public, and certainly with the political rhetoric one hears every October—especially in even-numbered years—which conveys the sense that crime rates are getting out of hand and that

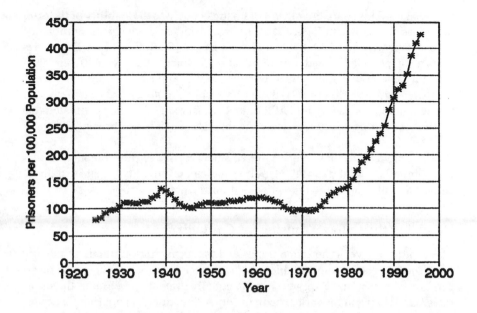

Figure 1.2 U.S. incarceration rate: State and federal prisoners.

SOURCE: Blumstein, A. (1988). U.S. criminal justice conundrum: Rising prison populations and stable crime rates. *Crime and Delinquency, 44*(1), 127-135.

the public demands an increasingly aggressive response. It is particularly noteworthy that the rhetoric and the associated perceptions have not diminished in recent years even though both robbery and murder rates have been on a steady decline.

Trends in Punishment

This general observation of stability in crime rates is in marked contrast to the recent trends in the incarceration rate. As shown in Figure 1.2, for the years from about 1923 to 1973, the United States had an incarceration rate that was itself strikingly stable at 110 persons per 100,000 with a coefficient of variation (the standard deviation of the series divided by the mean of the series) of only 8%. This stable pattern in the United States was sufficiently impressive, and similar patterns were observed in a number of other nations, that Jacqueline Cohen and I were encouraged to write a paper in 1973 developing a theory describing this "stability of punishment" (Blumstein & Cohen, 1973).

Almost immediately after that paper was published, an exponential growth in incarceration began in the United States, which has continued for the ensuing two decades. This sharp growth is a dramatic contrast to the stability of the prior period, as also shown in Figure 1.2. The growth increased the incarceration rate from 110 persons per 100,000 to 445 persons per 100,000 in 1997. This represents a compounded growth rate of about 6.5% since the early 1970s. In 1997, the total federal and state prison population was almost 1,250,000 prisoners, compared with 198,000 twenty-five years earlier. Another third of that number are held in local jails. By mid-1998, the U.S. Bureau of Justice estimated that 1,802,496 persons were incarcerated in the nation's jails and prisons (Gilliard, 1999).

The United States has clearly entered a new regime of punishment and punishment policy—and possibly also of crime and criminality—that is dramatically different from that which prevailed for the previous 50 years.

Resolving the Crime-Punishment Conundrum

The contrast between the crime trends and the incarceration trends of the past two decades poses a complex dilemma: with such a dramatic increase in incarceration rate, why have we not seen an equally dramatic decline in the crime rates? Or, looking at the influence in the other direction, considering that crime rates have stayed within a fairly narrow band of about 10% to 15% of their means, why have there been major policy shifts that produce a dramatic growth in prison populations with little effect on crime rates?

First, we should recognize the major sources of the growth in prison populations. Figure 1.3 shows the trends in incarceration rates for the five major offense types found in the prison population in the United States: drugs, murder, robbery, assault, and burglary.

Although all of the offense types display upward trends, none shows as much significant growth as drug offenses, which increased tenfold over the 14-year period depicted. Drug offenses alone accounted for about 45% of the total growth in these five offense types. Thus, we might examine separately the anticipated impact of drug arrests in contrast to the other four predatory offenses.

Drug-Offense Prisoners

Examining the impact on the crime rate of incarcerating drug offenders is rather complex. First, we do not anticipate a large impact on drug transactions, largely because the drug marketeers will simply recruit replacements for anyone deterred or incarcerated. Too often these replacements are young sellers who have to arm themselves with guns to protect themselves against the predators who populate the environment in which drug markets flourish. And the armed drug sellers inevitably trigger an arms race among those who operate in their

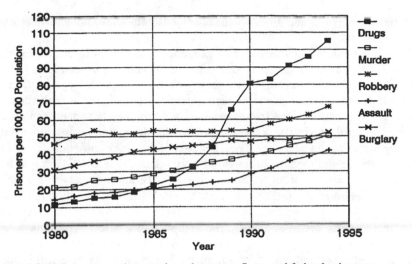

Figure 1.3 U.S. incarceration rate by crime type: State and federal prisoners.

SOURCE: Blumstein, A. (1988). U.S. criminal justice conundrum: Rising prison populations and stable crime rates. *Crime and Delinquency, 44*(1), 127-135.

neighborhoods. That arms race can diffuse well beyond where it begins, into other neighborhoods.

We might reasonably consider that the incarceration of a drug offender will contribute to the reduction of other kinds of crimes. If he is a crime "generalist," that is, one who engages in a variety of crimes, then we can anticipate the incapacitation of some of those other crimes while he is in prison. Indeed, there is some evidence developed by Cohen, Nagin, and colleagues (1998) that people convicted of drug possession have prior records comparable to those convicted of robbery or burglary. On the other hand, some fraction of the drug offense prisoners—and perhaps especially those convicted of *selling* drugs—may merely be entrepreneurs who would not be committing the more predatory crimes if they were in the community. In any event, the rapid growth in incarceration for drug offenses must be an inefficient means of achieving the side benefits of predatory crime reduction.

Predatory-Offense Prisoners

Whatever uncertainties there may be about drug-offense prisoners, over half of the growth in the prison population is associated with the four predatory offense. However, the two we chose to examine in Figure 1.1—robbery and murder, the most serious and probably the best measured—have not shown any significant reduction.

The most evident candidate for an exogenous factor that forced a growth in crime is crack cocaine, as it pervaded many of the nation's urban areas. Indeed, the reversal of the crime rate decline seen in the early 1980s is largely attributed to the influence of crack as a stimulus for crime, primarily because the demand for drugs generates a need for money to buy drugs, and that need can lead to crime, primarily property crime or robbery by those unable to earn needed money in the regular economy. Thus, because of the crack epidemic, the growth rate in murder and robbery following the trough in the mid-1980s might have been steeper were it not for the widespread incarceration already in place.

Yet it is entirely possible that the great expansion of incarceration resulted in some counterproductive consequences which diminished or counteracted the anticipated crime control benefits. The incapacitative effects could have been diminished because the marginal prisoners brought into prison during the expansion had lower frequencies of offending than their predecessors. It is possible that the criminogenic effects of incarceration outweighed or at least partially compensated for the incapacitative effects. And it is further possible that the great expansion of imprisonment has diminished prison's deterrent effect by eroding its stigma component.

There have been many attempts to estimate the incapacitation effect of incarceration. One of the most widely discussed efforts (Zedlewski, 1987) applies estimates of offender frequency derived from inmate surveys to additional offenders who might be incarcerated in U.S. prisons with an increase in sanction policy. This calculation leads to an extremely high value of estimated benefit per prisoner incarcerated, and is used by many to argue for much greater use of imprisonment.

Other work (Canela-Cacho, Blumstein, & Cohen, 1997), however, shows that there can be an order-of-magnitude difference between the offending frequency of robbers or burglars in prison compared with robbers or burglars on the outside. This large difference is explained by the fact that high-frequency offenders take chances more often and therefore have the highest risk of incarceration. As a result, high-frequency offenders are disproportionately represented in prisons, so the marginal offender would not be posing the same risk when counted among an expanded prison population.

Additionally, most analyses of incapacitation effects fail to take adequate account of criminal-career termination, and the consequent "wastage" of prison capacity (at least from the viewpoint of incapacitation) associated with prisoners who are still in prison after their criminal careers would have terminated. This effect of career termination is particularly important when long sentences (and especially those extreme sentences imposed under three strikes laws) are administered, because the likelihood of the career being terminated while in prison increases as the period of incarceration increases.

Incapacitation theory generally ignores any post-release consequences—either positive or negative—associated with the period of incarceration. It is likely that the period of incarceration will change post-release behavior. It could do so in pro-social terms through the mechanism of "rehabilitation," although this has largely disappeared from the set of purposes of incarceration in the U.S. criminal justice system. But it could also do so by creating a more crime-prone releasee.

This negative or "criminogenic" effect of incarceration can move the prisoner to a more serious level of criminal activity which shows itself in an expanded repertoire of crime that includes more serious kinds of offenses than he committed before, impelling him to commit them at a higher rate or lengthening the duration of his criminal career. All are clearly possible as a result of association with other more serious offenders (in what has been described as a "graduate school for crime"), or because of the debilitating stigma associated with having been a prisoner. That stigma, through some mixture of self-definition and others' response, could make it particularly difficult or impossible to find employment in the legitimate economy.

These criminogenic effects are most likely to occur in individuals who are incarcerated for drug offenses, and particularly those we have characterized as "entrepreneurs," who are much more likely to emerge from prison with more generalized criminal patterns than they had when they entered.

Another presumed major effect of sanction policy is the deterrence of criminal acts. Indeed, some advocates see punishment in ways quite similar to the way supply-side economists see the Laffer curve: they believe that we can achieve enough deterrent threat through the imposition of sufficiently severe sanctions that we would not have to impose the sanctions. Then, we would have less crime and even less incarceration. If that possibility were empirically true, it would certainly be an attractive policy option to consider. Unfortunately, however, there is considerable variability in the population of offenders or potential offenders to be deterred by the threat of criminal sanction. People with middle-class values and middle-class opportunities, especially those with no prior criminal record, are readily deterred from engaging in crime, particularly if they see a clear risk of being caught and convicted.

Indeed, it is probably fair to presume that much of the politicization of criminal justice sanction policy, which involves escalating sanction levels, attributes middle-class values to offenders. So, if certain criminal activity persists in the face of a mandatory-minimum sentence of 5 years, then the response is more often raising that mandatory minimum to 10 years, rather than questioning why the lower sanction has not been effective. These middle-class perspectives, which dominate so much of criminal justice policy, presume that such sanctions will work to deter others equally.

This problem of differential deterability is particularly apparent for crimes involving individuals who see no particular options in the legitimate economy, for whom life in the street is very risky anyway, and who have not been effectively socialized against committing crimes. For these, the prospect of spending time in prison, perhaps with others they know, of being assured meals and a bed (even if well short of luxurious), may not be strong enough to inhibit their criminal activity. Even though prison may not be a very attractive option, its increment of pain is likely to be far less than it is to middle-class populations.

This difficulty of deterrence is further exacerbated when large parts of a reference population are convicted or imprisoned. One important component of deterrence is the stigma associated with the sanction, but the stigma diminishes considerably when one's reference group already widely carries that stigma. Thus, the large degree of incarceration (e.g., a recent projection estimated that 29% of black males in the United States will experience imprisonment some time in their lives) can be counterproductive in attaining the deterrence that is an important part of its objective.

Some Further Research Needs

The effects of the dramatic changes in the application of punishment over the last 20 years are not easily analyzed. No single study has been definitive. It is probably reasonable to anticipate that there would have been some increase in crime based on exogenous considerations like the drug epidemic and the increasing isolation of inner cities from social and economic opportunities. Yet it is equally reasonable that sanctions have brought counterproductive consequences to incarceration. The study of these developments presents an important research agenda, the pursuit of which would give us a much better sense of the many factors that contribute to changes in crime rates, and particularly of the role of punishment in that process.

Note

1. A similar version of this article was first published as: U.S. criminal justice conundrum: Rising prison populations and stable crime rates, in *Crime and Delinquency,* January 1998, 44(1), 127-135, Sage Publications, and is reprinted with the author's permission.

References

Blumstein, A., & Cohen, J. (1973). A theory of the stability of punishment. *Journal of Criminal Law and Criminology, 64,* 198-206.

Canela-Cacho, J., Blumstein, A., & Cohen, J. (1997). Relationship between the offending frequency of imprisoned and free offenders. *Criminology, 35*(1), 133-175.

Cohen, J., Nagin, D., Wallstrom, G., & Wasserman, L. (1998). Hierarchical Bayesian analysis of arrest rates. *Journal of the American Statistical Association, 93*(444), 1260-1270.

Gilliard, D. K. (1999, March). *Prison and jail inmates at midyear 1998* (Bureau of Justice Statistics Bulletin No. NCJ-173414). Washington, DC: Government Printing Office.

Zedlewski, E. W. (1987). *Making confinement decisions.* (National Institute of Justice Research in Brief.) Washington, DC: U.S. Department of Justice.

Today's Violence

Khalid R. Pitts

Across the land, waves of violence seem to crest and break, terrorizing Americans in cities and suburbs, in prairie towns and mountain hollows. The President warns the nation: "Crime is increasing. Confidence in rigid and speedy justice is decreasing." Among urban children aged 10 to 14, homicides are up 150%, robberies are up 192%, assaults up 290%.

A national commission on violence describes the nation's fears: "To millions of Americans few things are more pervasive, more frightening, more real today than violent crime . . . The fear of being victimized by criminal attack has touched us all in some new way." And a Senate committee describes surging violence in Washington, D.C.: "Innocent and unoffending persons are shot, stabbed and otherwise shamefully maltreated, and not infrequently the offender is not even arrested."

Violence is indeed relentless. But in America, it has always been so. The first quotation is from the 1929 inaugural speech of Herbert Hoover. The children's crime figures are from 1967. The second quotation is from the Commission on the Causes and Prevention of Violence. The year was 1968. And the Senate report on crime in Washington was issued in 1860.

The paragraphs above first appeared on the front page of the Philadelphia Inquirer in 1994, written by reporter David Zucchino (Zucchino, 1994, p. 1) at a time when national polls revealed Americans perceived crime as the most important problem facing the country (Maguire & Pasteore, 1997) (see Figure 2.1).

As Zucchino noted, American history has always been steeped in violence: This is a country born of revolution, torn by civil war, and altered by urban unrest. Through rebellions, riots, lynchings, and drive-by shootings (first performed by bootleggers of the 1920s), each generation has left its mark on America's legacy of violence. A presidential crime commission reported in 1968 that "virtually every generation since the founding of the Nation and before has felt

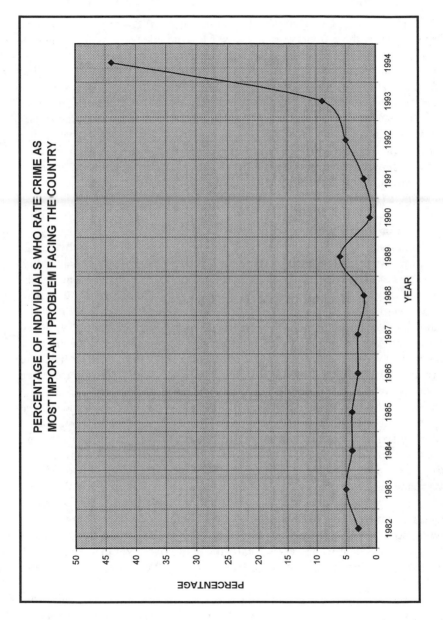

PERCENTAGE OF INDIVIDUALS WHO RATE CRIME AS MOST IMPORTANT PROBLEM FACING THE COUNTRY

SOURCEBOOK OF CRIMINAL JUSTICE STATISTICS

itself threatened by the specter of rising crime and violence" (Zucchino, 1994, p. 22).

The crime sprees of early 1990s, Zucchino argued, differed in only two primary ways from those of previous periods: More people were dying, primarily because of gun usage, and the average age of both perpetrators and victims was younger than ever before. Indeed, a 1998 victimization survey found that violence-related crime rates among the general population have been relatively stable over the last 35 years, and in fact decreased in 1997 (Rand, Zawitz, & Maltz, 1998). Yet one would get the opposite impression from watching television news or reading most major newspapers. Today's technology enables the public frequently to witness violence up close. Ratings-driven television newscasts report on murders and other violent crimes, while the airwaves are saturated with "in your face" reality-based shows documenting violent crimes and cop killings (Zucchino, 1994, p. 22). No previous generation of Americans has been subjected to such a plethora of violence-related material, packaged either as news or as entertainment.

Criminologists Zimring and Hawkins explained the phenomenon by recognizing that Americans use the terms "crime" and "violence" interchangeably. Americans express concern about "the crime problem" or "the violence problem" as if they were the same thing. But it is really lethal violence that they fear. The notion of runaway crime in the United States stems from the fact that those committing assaults or robberies frequently do so with firearms. Lethal violence is indeed an American problem, and citizens fear the prospect of lethal violence more than any crime. The public's fear of burglary, for example, is fueled more by images of possible physical harm than by what usually takes place when prowlers enter mostly unoccupied dwellings (Zimring & Hawkins, 1997).

Specifically, it is the increased use of firearms to commit crimes and resolve disputes, rather than an actual increase in violence, that makes America so deadly. Fights and arguments are more lethal today than ever, as combatants are more often armed. Disputes, not meant to be crimes and once settled with fists or knives, now end with gunfire. In fact, a 1993 victimization survey found that firearms were involved in 29% of violent crimes involving rape, sexual assault, robbery, and aggravated assault (Zawitz, 1995, p. 1). In 1997, the FBI estimated that approximately 68% of all homicides were committed with a firearm (Fox & Zawitz, 1999). Increasingly, it is the young who are becoming the victims of these types of violent crimes, and virtually the entire rise in youth homicides and the subsequent fear of violent crime has been propelled by gunfire (see Figure 2.2).

In response to the rise in lethality, the public and politicians have made a conscious decision to address the complex problem of violence with broad applications of an old and seemingly simple remedy: prison. Consequently, the late 1980s and 1990s witnessed an unprecedented rise in jail and prison populations,

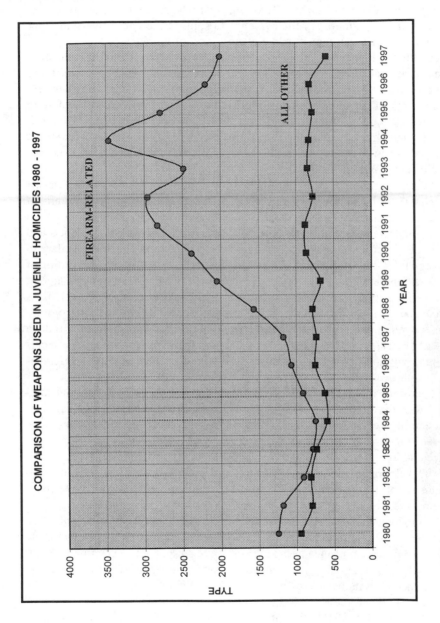

COMPARISON OF WEAPONS USED IN JUVENILE HOMICIDES 1980 - 1997

FIREARM-RELATED

ALL OTHER

Source: FBI, Supplementary Homicide Reports: 1976-97

mostly for nonviolent offenses. Historically, public support has strongly favored the expansion of prisons, particularly during cycles of real or perceived violence, even though there is little evidence to support the belief that imprisonment has a significant impact on the overall level of violence.

It was not until 20 years into prison expansion, in the late 1990s, that the incidence of violent offenses began to decline. Few criminologists place primary credit for this drop with the increase in prison populations. Rather, they have explained some of the decrease on the improved economy, the availability of more prevention programs, improved policing strategies, better security and surveillance technology, a flooded consumer market creating less demand for stolen goods, and even on an increase in access to credit cards, which decreases the carrying of cash (Witkin, 1998).

At the same time, the crack cocaine fad and its associated increase in gun carrying has diminished in many major cities. Although policing and imprisonment played a role in stemming the crack problem, some analysis found that police sweeps and incarceration sometimes, in fact, resulted in more violence and homicide in certain neighborhoods by creating a vacuum for other dealers to fight and fill (Goldstein, 1994). The predominant theory explaining the fading of the crack epidemic and its ensuing violence credits the development among most young people of a strong social norm against it (Wiktin, 1998, p. 30). As demand decreases, a perception of safety is propagated throughout the community. As young people believe that their neighborhoods are safer, they reduce their gun carrying. As a few individuals abandon their guns, a contagion effect is created, with multiplicative responses throughout in the community (Hemenway, Prothrow-Stith, Bergstein, Ander, & Kennedy, 1996).

Support for approaches to curbing violence, however, has been minimal compared with the support for correctional systems. Prevention programs are seldom endorsed even though certain model programs have been shown to reduce crime. Programs that focus on the prevention of child abuse and neglect, enhance children's intellectual and social development, provide support and guidance to vulnerable adolescents, and counsel juvenile offenders have demonstrated effectiveness (Currie, 1998, p. 81). Yet committing resources to these programs is unpopular, because their results are not often immediate.

Throughout our history, Americans have always valued incarceration and punishment as solutions for the crime problem. Few emotions resonate more with the public than vengeance and the desire to strike back at criminals. As far back as the 1960s, a Gallup poll found that "large numbers of Americans felt that making penalties more severe, giving the police a freer hand, and increasing the size of the police force were the most relevant steps toward reduction of crime" (Zucchino, 1994, p. 22). Politicians have favored the "three strikes" legislation since the 1920s, and "get tough" measures proposing more prisons, more police, and longer sentences are an enduring response to crime waves.

Most criminologists agree that few of our "get tough" measures have made any substantial difference in lethal violence. Yet policymakers prefer to wait for an alarm of violence to sound, and then respond with another tough approach so that they are seen as decisive and hard-hitting. And the public is quick to sound that alarm—unnerved by the sensationalistic image of the latest "stone-cold killer" brought to them by mainstream media. Each best get ready for more: policymakers and the public must be prepared for a whole new generation of young people.

References

Currie, E. (1998). *Crime and punishment in America.* New York: Metropolitan Books.

FBI. (1998). *Supplimentary homicide reports, 1976-97.* Available on-line at http://www. ojp.usdoj.gov/bjs/homicide/homtrnd.htm

Fox, J. A., & Zawitz, M. (1999). *Homicide trends in the United States.* (Bureau of Justice Statistics Special Report.) [On-line]. Available: http://www.ojp.usdoj.gov/bjs/pub/pdf/htius.pdfv

Goldstein, P. J. (1994, June). *Analysis of drugs and homicide.* Proceedings of the Third Annual Spring Symposium of the Homicide Research Working Group. (National Institute of Justice, Research Report.) Washington, DC: U.S. Department of Justice.

Hemenway, D., Prothrow-Stith, D., Bergstein, J., Ander, R., & Kennedy, B. P. (1996). Gun carrying among adolescents. *Law and Contemporary Problems, 59* (1), 39-51.

Maguire, K., & Pasteore, A. L. (Eds.). (1997). *Sourcebook of criminal justice statistics 1996.* U.S. Department of Justice, Bureau of Justice Statistics. Washington, DC: Government Printing Office.

Rand, M. R., Zawitz, M., & Maltz, M. (1998). *Criminal victimization 1997, changes 1996-97 with trends 1993-97.* (Bureau of Justice Statistics Special Report, NCJ-173385.) [On-line]. Available: www.ojp.usdoj.gov/bjs/pub/pdf/cv97.pdf.

Witkin, G. (1998, May 25). The crime bust. *U.S. News and World Report, 124* (20), 28-40.

Zawitz, M. (1995). *Guns used in crime: Firearms, crime, and criminal justice.* (Bureau of Justice Statistics Special Report, NCJ-148201.) [On-line]. Available: http://www. ojp.usdoj.gov/bjs/pub/pdf/guic.pdf.

Zimring, F. E., & Hawkins, G. (1997). *Crime is not the problem: Lethal violence in America.* New York: Oxford University Press.

Zucchino, D. (1994, October 30). Today's violent crime is old story with a twist. *The Philadelphia Inquirer,* pp. 1, 22.

and used labor as its instrument by making it degrading, painful, and endless. They forced inmates to wear striped uniforms bearing the word "convict" and to be chained together and chained to posts. By the late 1800s, as one prison expert observed, some southern prisons operated not unlike slavery. In these prisons, in which blacks made up more than 75% of inmates, prisoners were leased to entrepreneurs who organized them into chain gangs under the watch of armed (white) guards to perform their work (Edgardo, 1995, p. 176). Many of these practices did little to stop crime, reform offenders, or deter violence; instead they created hostile environments scandalized by frequent abuses.

As a result, in the latter part of the 1900s, the courts intervened and made many dramatic changes to the ways in which prisons and jails operate. Recognizing that constitutional standards applied even to institutionalized persons, the law demanded closer scrutiny and accountability from jail and prison management. The incarceration itself was to be the punishment, not an occasion for the state to arbitrarily inflict additional punishment. Around the same time, it was recognized that the mere incarceration and warehousing of inmates provided little benefit to society, so support grew for inmate programming such as substance abuse treatment, education, and vocational training. Former U.S. Chief Justice Warren Burger stated: "We must accept the reality that to confine offenders behind walls without trying to change them is an expensive folly with short-term benefits—winning the battles while losing the war" (Taylor, 1993, p. 90).

Today, however, the pendulum is swinging back to the philosophy of punishment. Many now believe that the more people we incarcerate, the longer we incarcerate them, the worse we make their conditions of confinement, and the more we humiliate and degrade them, the less likely they will be to commit another crime. We have entered into an era of vindictiveness or "get even" punishment, masked by a theme of "getting tough." Some jurisdictions have reinstated chain gangs, chain posts, and the old striped convict uniforms. Others have removed air conditioners from facilities. Some have eliminated incentives for good behavior, abolished educational programs, and so on. Nearly every state is constructing a "supermax" prison, which is basically a direct descendant of the Eastern State Penitentiary but with an important difference: Now isolation is meant to be punitive, not redemptive.

None of these strategies can be expected to significantly affect crime and violence in our country. We are greatly mistaken by relying on incarceration to solve such problems. In fact, incarceration often contributes to the problems. For example, graduates of several juvenile boot camps, programs which recently became widely popular partly because of their perceived toughness, were found to be more involved in subsequent crime than graduates of traditional programs (Sherman et al., 1997, p. 9-30). As another example, many juveniles are currently not provided educational activities while incarcerated. Given the strong link between low levels of education and high rates of criminal activity, it is not surprising that so many juveniles remain involved in the criminal justice system well into their adult lives (Center on Crime, Communities, and Culture, 1997).

As it turns out, education is a good example of programming that can turn the incarceration experience into a gain for society. The Texas Department of Criminal Justice found that criminal recidivism for its degree holders leaving their system between September 1990 and August 1991 was 15%, four times lower than the general recidivism rate of 60%. The higher the level of degree, the lower the rate of recidivism (Tracy & Johnson, 1994, p. 7). Several other states have shown similar results.

Certainly, there are some people for whom lengthy and no-frills incarceration is appropriate and necessary. These are the people who commit vicious, remorseless violent acts, whose victims suffer tremendous pain and anguish, and who continuously present a threat to the general public. Incarceration might not help them, but it will make us safer. Yet in terms of the numbers of offenders and the numbers of crimes committed, such violent felons are the minority of our incarcerated population.

Today's corrections reality is such: the fastest growing jail populations are those captured from our "war on drugs," the deinstitutionalization of our mental health system, and mandatory minimum sentencing policies. Thus, our correctional institutions consist of a very large number of nonviolent convicted misdemeanants and felons, a very large number of pretrial detainees who haven't been convicted of anything, a large number of persons suffering from serious mental illness, and only a minority of violent offenders. Moreover, the majority of our prisoners are chronic substance abusers, functionally illiterate, indigent, or possess few, if any, job skills. The current systems provide less and less of the direction prisoners need to become productive.

That is not to suggest that punishment has no place for offenders. In fact, punishment and restitution are integral to the whole puzzle. People must accept responsibility for their life choices and be held accountable for their actions. However, punishment must be swift, sure, and reasonable, and be accompanied by attempts to foster positive change in behavior. Punishing because it makes us feel good or gives us some odd sense of pleasure is perverse and pointless.

What is the charge to jail and prison administrators? What does it mean for a jail or prison to do a good job? Is it to prevent escapes and keep the inmates apart from society as much as possible? Is it to render punishments that deter the inmate from ever repeating an offense? Is it to issue punishments that satisfy the vengeance of society? Is it to transform the inmate into a productive citizen? Is it to serve as a general deterrent? The answers from society or its politicians have never been clear or consistent, yet jail and prison administrators must struggle with changing mandates. One charge, however, is clear: No one wants inmates to become worse. And yet, this is what happens most frequently.

We cannot incarcerate our way out of our crime and violence. Jails and prisons have a role, but are only pieces of a much larger strategy required to prevent crime and improve public safety. Some programming, given the right population and right delivery, rehabilitates and reforms prisoners. Other programming is ineffective, and sometimes counterproductive. We must consider that, of those who are incarcerated in our jails and prisons today, tens of thousands will be back in our communities tomorrow and every day thereafter. The choice is whether we want them back in the same, better, or worse condition than when they left.

References

The Center on Crime, Communities, and Culture. (1997). *Education as crime prevention* (Research Brief No. 2). New York: Author.

Edgardo, R. (1995). The failure of reform. In N. Morris & D. Rothman (Eds.), *The Oxford history of prison.* New York: Oxford University Press.

Johnston, N. (1994). *Eastern State Penitentiary: Crucible of good intentions.* Philadelphia: University of Pennsylvania Press.

Rothman, D. J. (1995). Perfecting the prison. In N. Morris & D. Rothman (Eds.), *The Oxford history of prison.* New York: Oxford University Press.

Sherman, L. W., Gottfredson, D., MacKenzie, D., Eck, J., Reuter, P., & Bushway, S. (1997). *Preventing crime: What works, what doesn't, what's promising* (NCJ 165366). Washington, DC: U.S. Department of Justice, Office of Justice Programs, National Institute of Justice.

Taylor, J. M. (1993, January 25). Pell Grants for prisoners. *The Nation.*

Tracy, C., & Johnson, C. (1994). *Review of various outcome studies relating prison education to reduced recidivism.* Huntsville, TX: Windham School System.

4

Prisoner Rehabilitation
Feeling Better but Getting Worse?

Colleen R. McLaughlin

Figure 4.1a A collection of prison-made knives recovered during searches of inmates in the Texas Department of Criminal Justice. Weapons are constructed using any possible material, such as utensils, door jambs, razors, and vent covers.

Photograph courtesy of the Texas Department of Criminal Justice. Reprinted with permission.

Figure 4.1b An art object built by an inmate in the Texas Department of Criminal Justice using rolled magazine pages, yarn from socks, and shoe polish.

Photograph by John P. May.

In the rush to incarcerate, very little attention has been paid to what programs or treatments actually work. There is seldom an attempt to evaluate the efficacy of the programs, even though the potential impact on public safety may be enormous. When offenders recidivate, they frequently are blamed, yet ineffective or even detrimental prison programs are rarely considered.

Federal regulations for the Protection of Human Subjects (45 CFR 46) are extended to prisoners due to past abuses and the concern that prisoners may be limited in their ability to give truly informed consent (Anno, 1991). Consequently, testing of biomedical treatments or medications on incarcerated individuals requires proper review for potential deleterious effects, appropriate consent procedures, and strict requirements for monitoring and outcome evaluation. Behavioral interventions designed to reduce criminal offending, on the other hand, are developed and conducted frequently by people with little or no training in the area, no monitoring or thought as to the potential damage that an intervention may cause, and no informed consent. Such untested "treatment" programs could arguably be considered unauthorized and uncontrolled experiments on prisoners. There is often no benefit of external review, monitoring, or informed consent as required with other experiments on confined populations. The treatment of sex offenders provides a concrete example of the different standards afforded biomedical treatment and rehabilitative programming. The biomedical treatments thus far considered, including chemical castration, remain highly scrutinized and controversial while rehabilitative programming may remain largely unregulated.

Furthermore, concerns about the validity of informed consent and the right to refuse treatment emerge with respect to rehabilitative services provided to offender populations. Incentives such as improved living conditions and freedom from boredom and danger are powerful inducements for individuals in confined settings. These inducements may be sufficiently strong as to compromise an inmate's ability to weigh the potential risks and benefits of participation in a given program, thereby compromising a true informed consent. Additional concern for the potential of coercion arises when participation in rehabilitative services is linked to the inmate's length of stay. Finally, related to a limited view of prisoners' rights has been the relatively recent proliferation of rehabilitative programs with a thin veneer of "treatment" over a strong punitive core. These trends are reflected in the interest of restorative justice, as well as the reemergence of chain gangs. Again, many of these programs have little or no demonstrated efficacy, and some have been found to be detrimental when applied to the wrong population (Sherman et al., 1997).

Like biomedical treatments, some programs work, others do not, and some make people worse. Scientific research has documented prison programs in which the unintended outcomes include increases in criminal behavior (Sherman et al., 1997). In these extreme examples, correctional settings are truly unhealthy environments. For example, it has been recognized that, rather than serving as places of punishment, correctional facilities may also serve as training schools for criminal offending. In addition, describing, reliving, or reenacting the offense, as some treatment programs advocate, may possess significant secondary gain for some patterns of offending. These activities may afford the offender an opportunity to "critique" the offense, to learn from past mistakes, and have the potential to glamorize the pattern of offending.

Programs found to increase criminal recidivism can be divided into two categories. The first includes programs that result in increases in recidivism due to increased monitoring. In other words, the closer an offender's behavior is watched, the more likely it is that a violation (often only a technical violation) will be caught, which might otherwise have been missed or even ignored with less intensive supervision (Sherman et al., 1997). The second category of program failures, however, includes those programs that are truly criminogenic. For example, some gang intervention programs have been found to increase actual rates of criminal offending, which were subsequently reduced when the program was terminated (Sherman et al., 1997). External pressure applied by the intervention on the gang increased criminal activity by increasing cohesiveness of the group. Similarly, segregating or grouping offenders for intensive treatment programming may have the unintended consequence of glamorizing a relatively prestigious pattern of offending (e.g., drug trafficking), as well as providing offenders an opportunity to learn, build alliances, and network. Finally, "Scared Straight," shock probation or parole programs, and certain boot camps have been associated with increases in recidivism among young offenders (Sherman et al., 1997). Interaction with incarcerated offenders may be particularly attractive to high-risk youth who may view involvement in criminal offending as glamorous and attempt to emulate the offenders involved in the program.

Individuals or correctional systems finding these "criminogenic" outcomes may be reluctant to report or disseminate their findings due to fear of litigation from the offenders, their victims, or both for these unintended outcomes. The reporting of all outcome data, whether good or bad, is essential to the provision of beneficial rehabilitative services, ultimately ensuring public safety. This is especially critical when a program description and outline have been widely distributed prior to thorough outcome evaluation, as is frequently the case. Dissemination of outcome data becomes imperative in the face of treatment failure to ensure that others implementing the same or similar programs are aware of the outcome and potential risks associated with a particular intervention. Stringent requirements for thorough review, monitoring, and outcome evaluation of all "experimental" treatment protocols, as well as the assurance of truly informed consent, may serve to attenuate these concerns.

Another danger of ineffective rehabilitative programming relates to what might best be described as a false sense of security when an offender is released after "treatment." Given the significant public safety concerns intrinsically linked to the success of the programs, it follows that unflinching evaluation should be the norm rather than the exception. Determining what works, when, and for whom would permit the judicious allocation of scarce programmatic resources. Direct benefits of this approach would be the potential for enhanced public safety through reduced recidivism, as well as the recapture of lost lives and the opportunity to return offenders to the community as productive citizens.

In summary, the lack of monitoring and evaluation of rehabilitative programming in the correctional setting has essentially resulted in the proliferation of what may best be described as large social experiments, with the lives of prisoners as well as overall public safety at stake. Although it may be difficult to predict individual behavior upon release from confinement, thorough outcome evaluation provides an opportunity to make general predictions regarding the likelihood of recidivism for program participants. "Good intentions are not enough" (Sherman et al., 1997, p. 3-19). When evaluation is limited or nonexistent it becomes impossible to know what works. Consequently, determinations related to likelihood of recidivism become increasingly difficult and this poses a threat to public safety.

References

Anno, B. J. (1991). *Prison health care: Guidelines for the management of an adequate delivery system.* Chicago: National Commission on Correctional Health Care.

Sherman, L. W., Gottfredson, D., MacKenzie, D., Eck, J., Reuter, P., & Bushway, S. (1997). *Preventing crime: What works, what doesn't, what's promising* (NCJ 165366). Washington, DC: U.S. Department of Justice, Office of Justice Programs, National Institute of Justice.

5

Criminalizing Addictions

Roger H. Peters

The Criminalization of Drug Offenders

The most important factor contributing to the growth of prison populations is the significant rise in the number of drug offenders sentenced to prison, including a 478% increase in drug offenders committed to state prisons and a 545% increase to federal prisons from 1985 to 1996 (Mumola & Beck, 1997). The "war on drugs" has been waged by making prisoners of drug users and sellers. Across the country, new construction for jails and prisons has severely strained local and state budgets and has reduced monies available for education, public health, and substance abuse prevention and treatment programs. As much is spent each year to incarcerate federal drug offenders as for all drug education and prevention efforts (Drug Strategies, 1996).

Leading to the surge of drug offenders committed to prison are changes in law enforcement practices, in sentencing law and policy, and in policies regarding release from incarceration. Since 1985, law enforcement has targeted street-level users and sellers through various drug "sting" and "reverse sting" operations, leading to significantly more arrests and convictions for drug possession and sales. The Sentencing Reform Act of 1984 has also had a major impact by abolishing parole for federal offenders and limiting sentence reductions for good behavior. Many state and federal prisoners incarcerated for drug offenses are no longer eligible for parole and must serve mandatory minimum sentences as a result of legislation such as the Anti-Drug Abuse Act passed in 1986 and related state legislation. Legislative initiatives to "get tough" on drugs included the Violent Crime Control and Law Enforcement Act of 1994, which was the most extensive crime bill in the history of the United States (U.S. Department of

Justice, 1997), and included a variety of enhanced sentences for drug offenders. The "zero tolerance" policies reflected in legislation and law enforcement strategies and "user accountability" statutes implemented at state and local levels further expanded the war on drugs from suppliers and dealers to users as well. By 1994, 65% of those arrested for drug possession were incarcerated and spent an average of 44 months in prison (Maguire & Pastore, 1995).

The prevailing assumption in the expansion of law enforcement and legislative efforts has been that, by targeting drug users, demand for drugs would be reduced, thus making drug trafficking less profitable and reducing supply. However, most regular drug users are clearly unable to reduce their habit without outside assistance, despite the enhanced risks of arrest and no matter what potential penalties they face (Greenwood, 1995). For example, in the 5 years after LSD was criminalized, the number of active users nevertheless increased from a few thousand to an estimated 5 million (Courtwright, 1992). In summarizing the effects of sanctions on recidivism, Fagan (1994) notes that drug sales and use are "persistent and somewhat intractable behaviors that are as likely to be deterred by probation as by imprisonment" (p. 202).

Addictions and Prisoners

Approximately 23% of state inmates and 60% of federal inmates are currently incarcerated on drug-related offenses (Mumola & Beck, 1997). The increasing population of drug offenders in prisons is disproportionately African American, reflecting sentencing policies and expanded law enforcement initiatives targeting inner-city areas. A significant number of drug offenders committed to prison are arrested for low-level offenses (e.g., drug possession, sales of small quantities of drugs) that do not involve sophisticated criminal activity, and have no prior history of violence or arrest (Maguire & Pastore, 1995). This group of offenders is more often female, Hispanic, have higher educational levels, and display fewer behavioral problems in prison than other inmates (Drug Strategies, 1996).

Nonviolent drug offenders are often imprisoned due to mandatory minimum sentences and an absence of community diversion programs that involve supervision and treatment. Most nonviolent drug offenders would fare better in community-based treatment centers or "alternatives to incarceration" programs that do not require the costly level of security and supervision provided in prisons (Center for Substance Abuse Treatment, 1995; Join Together, 1996).

Many prisoners, even if not incarcerated specifically for a drug-related offense, have a substance use or dependence disorder. The prevalence rates of substance use disorders in prisons are significantly greater than in the general population. Approximately 56% of prisoners have a diagnosable drug use disorder, and 25% have an alcohol use disorder (Robins & Regier, 1991), yet few have pre-

Federal Bureau of Prisons. (1998, February). *Triad drug treatment evaluation six-month report: Executive summary.* Washington, DC: U.S. Department of Justice.

Field, G. (1989). *A study of the effects of intensive treatment on reducing the criminal recidivism of addicted offenders.* Salem, OR: Oregon Department of Corrections.

Field, G. (1992). Oregon Prison Drug Treatment programs. In C. Leukefeld & F. Tims (Eds.), *Drug abuse treatment in prisons and jails* (Research Monograph Series, Vol. 118., pp. 142-155). Rockville, MD: National Institute on Drug Abuse.

Gerstein, D. R., Harwood, H. J., Suter, N., & Malloy, K. (1994). *Evaluating recovery services: The California Drug and Alcohol Treatment Assessment (CALDATA), general report.* Sacramento, CA: California Department of Alcohol and Drug Programs.

Greenwood, P. (1995). Strategies for improving communication between enforcement and treatment efforts in controlling illegal drug use. *Journal of Drug Issues, 25*(1), 73-87.

Harlow, C. W. (1992). *Drug enforcement and treatment in prisons* (Special report). Washington, DC: U.S. Department of Justice, Bureau of Justice Statistics.

Join Together. (1996). *Fixing a filing system. National policy recommendations: How the criminal justice system should work with communities to reduce substance abuse* (Report from a Join Together Policy Panel). Boston, MA: Author.

Lipton, D. S. (1995). *The effectiveness of treatment for drug abusers under criminal justice supervision* (National Institute of Justice Research Report). Washington, DC: National Institute of Justice.

Maguire, K., & Pastore, A. L. (Eds.). (1995). *Sourcebook of criminal justice statistics—1994.* Washington, DC: U.S. Department of Justice, Bureau of Justice Statistics.

Martin, S. S., Butzin, C. A., & Inciardi, J. A. (1995). Assessment of a multistage therapeutic community for drug-involved offenders. *Journal of Psychoactive Drugs, 27*(1), 109-116.

Mumola, C. J., & Beck, A. J. (1997). *Prisoners in 1996* (NCJ-164619). Washington, DC: U.S. Department of Justice, Bureau of Justice Statistics.

National Center on Addiction and Substance Abuse. (1998). *Behind bars: Substance abuse and America's prison population* [On-line]. Retrieved July 5, 1999 from the World Wide Web at Http://www.casacolumbia.org/publications1456/publications_show.htm?doc_id=5745.

Peters, R. H., & Kearns, W. D. (1992). Drug abuse history and treatment needs of jail inmates. *American Journal of Drug and Alcohol Abuse, 18*(3), 355-366.

Robins, L. N., & Regier, D. A. (1991). *Psychiatric disorders in America: The epidemiologic catchment area study.* New York: Free Press.

Rydell, C. P., & Everingham, S. S. (1994). *Controlling cocaine: Supply versus demand programs.* Prepared for the Office of National Drug Control Policy, Drug Policy Research Center. Santa Monica, CA: RAND.

Simpson, D. D., Knight, K., & Pevoto, C. (1996). *Research summary: Focus on drug treatment in criminal justice settings.* Ft. Worth: Texas Christian University, Institute of Behavioral Research.

U.S. Department of Justice (1997). *Violent Crime Control and Law Enforcement Act of 1994* [On-line]. Retrieved July 1, 1999 from the World Wide Web at http://www.usdoj.gov/crime/crime.html

Wexler, H. K., Falkin, G. P., & Lipton, D. S. (1990). Outcome evaluation of a prison thera-
    peutic community for substance abuse treatment. *Criminal Justice and Behavior,*
    17(1), 71-92.
Wexler, H. K., Falkin, G. P., Lipton, D. S., & Rosenblum, A. B. (1992). Outcome evalua-
    tion of a prison therapeutic community for substance abuse treatment. In C. Leukefeld
    & F. Tims (Eds.), Drug abuse treatment in prisons and jails (pp. 156-175). *Research*
    Monograph Series, Vol. 118. Rockville, MD: National Institute on Drug Abuse.

6

Make 'em Break Rocks

Kenneth L. McGinnis

Over the last two decades, America has witnessed an ongoing campaign that promised to eradicate crime through policies promising maximum punishment and incapacitation. The results of this campaign are well known. The prison and jail populations of the United States have increased from approximately 500,000 to nearly 2 million persons, with an additional 3.8 million individuals on probation and parole. Even more staggering is the fact that 1 out of every 36 Americans is under the control of the criminal justice system.

While the debate over the effectiveness of this campaign of incapacitation to reduce crime and, more important, to reduce the fear of crime, rages throughout America, one thing is clear: The economic costs of imprisonment are enormous. In state after state, the desire to expand prison capacities has become embroiled in the reality that funding for education, social service programs, mental health services, and infrastructure improvements will have to be deferred or reduced to accommodate the growing corrections budgets. In Michigan, budgets for correctional programs grew from less than $300 million in 1980 to over $1.4 billion in 1998. One in every six dollars of state general revenue expenditures now goes to support prison, probation, and parole functions. The dominance of the corrections system in state government is even more evident in the fact that the Department of Corrections workforce of 16,500 represents one out of every four state employees.

The cost of incapacitation of our offenders has been enormous. In a time when moderates and conservatives have joined forces to reduce taxes and, at the same time, reduce the size of government, correctional systems are demanding huge increases in both operating budgets and the capital expenditures required to build new facilities. Law enforcement-minded officials in state after state are being forced to reconcile the competing interests of corrections and other needed state services. In 1995, Oklahoma state senator Carl Hobson noted that prisons had received larger increases than any other state agency. He observed that, ". . . It's getting more and more difficult to find enough money for every state need" (Gest, 1995, p. 24). In 1998, Michigan state senator John Schwarz, chairman of the Senate Appropriations Subcommittee for Higher Education, stated emphatically, "I won't vote for a corrections budget that has one penny more in new money than what goes to universities."[1] In California, the university system's capital expansion program was put on hold as billions of dollars were directed to pay for the construction of new prisons. Examples of this nature can be found in virtually every region of the country.

As the public continues to demand that something be done about the perception of runaway crime, politicians and public officials are refocusing attention on the cheaper and the more attention-grabbing issue of prison conditions and programs. Public officials everywhere have adopted the blunt philosophy of former Massachusetts Governor William Weld, who, in April 1998, at then Attorney General William Barr's *Summit on Corrections*, stated that life in prison should be ". . . akin to a walk through the fires of hell."[2]

Recognizing the fiscal reality that expansion of prisons, if left unchecked, will eventually bankrupt a state's ability to provide other needed services and programs, legislative and political leaders turned to this "get tough" approach to prison operations. The opinions of Michigan state representative Mike Goschka are reflective of attitudes nationally. During a debate on prisoner conditions he stated, "Prisoners have it too easy now. They got color TV's, weight lifting equipment, libraries. . . . We need to return to the concept that prison is not fun" (Cole, 1995, p. 6A). Many, like Rep. Goschka and Governor Weld, have adopted the theory that the most effective way to prevent crime is to make the punishment so harsh and so certain that those who are considering a life of crime will decide that the risk is not worth taking. The concept of these leaders is simple: Remove prison perks and save money while enhancing punishment. "Make 'em break rocks" has become a cornerstone in the criminal justice agenda for many elected officials. More important, it is viewed by a large segment of the public as an effective and appropriate means of fighting crime in the United States.

Examples of this strategy can be found across the county in almost every jurisdiction. In February 1998, the California Department of Corrections initiated steps to revoke a number of privileges, including weight lifting equipment. A spokesperson for then Governor Pete Wilson, in explaining the basis for many of the changes in policy, stated that prisoners are ". . . there to be punished, and hopefully rehabilitated. . . . They're not there to be entertained and catered to" (Morain, 1998). Similar debates occurred in Congress over the use of weights in the Federal Bureau of Prisons. In Michigan, state representative David Jaye advocated "hot bunking," the practice of sleeping in shifts on the same bunk. He stated that, "We could double the prisoner capacity at the existing prisons by instituting two different sleeping shifts" (Jaye, 1996, p. 5). A colleague of Jaye's introduced legislation that would ban television and radio from state prisons and all county jails. In introducing his legislation he cited Florida as a state that had already implemented such a ban on televisions.

In jurisdiction after jurisdiction, there has been a call to eliminate everything with the perception of being less than "tough." Law libraries, educational programs, weight lifting equipment, televisions, vocational training programs, access to medical care, food service, personal property, uniforms, and visits are among those aspects of prison life singled out in some way as needing to be reformed or eliminated in their entirety. At the same time, public officials have demanded implementation of chain gangs, pink uniforms, hard labor, hot bunking, food loafs (a loaf made of all foods prepared for that meal, served to prisoners who have thrown food at staff or other inmates), and other punitive measures.

Correctional administrators are caught squarely in the middle of this national debate. As prison populations have grown and double bunking (two or more prisoners in a cell) has become the norm, prisons have become more difficult to manage. Administrators have seen the need to evaluate every aspect of prison operations and to implement policies and procedures that address the new demands the changing population has placed on prison staff.

Reductions in personal property, revised visitation rules, and placing prisoners in uniforms are among the policy changes supported by a number of experienced correctional administrators. These measures are supported by administrators, however, not out of a desire to be punitive, but to enhance the safety and security of the facilities they manage. For example, restrictions in access to and quantities of personal property are necessitated by the size and demographics of the population. Changes based on sound, well thought out correctional policy are significantly different from legislative edicts based on the new "get tough" attitudes of many public officials. Correctional administrators must weigh the benefits of policy change against the potential impact these changes may have on the stability of the institutions they manage. Public officials often view the impact on the prison environment as secondary to their goal of providing a solution to a very complicated issue.

The modern prison environment is a complex and reactionary being. Change that is viewed as unwarranted and punitive is often met with resistance and, in the worst case, violence. Correctional administrators must consider that reality when implementing new policies. Public officials proposing tough measures often times neither understand nor are worried about the consequences. Don Novey, president of the California Correctional Peace Officers Association, expressed the concern of the correctional officers his union represents when he stated that "... You're massively overcrowded.... You're understaffed.... And this stuff goes to the forefront. It's stupid. But it resonates with the public. We get this perception that we're tough..." (Morain, 1998). Similarly, Pat Keohene, president of the North American Association of Wardens and Superintendents, expressed the frustration and concern of many correctional professionals when he said, "... When it comes to managing prisons, no one has all the answers, but someone should have the courtesy to seek our opinions before they pass these laws" (Clayton, 1997, p. 1).

The concern that we are attempting to resolve the issue of violence in America at the expense of creating violence and tension in our prisons is real. Many feel that these punitive measures place the correctional staff and the prisoners they manage at risk. But perhaps even more important is the potential that these measures have to increase the very problem they attempt to address. Will the toughening and hardening of our prisons actually create a meaner and more isolated offender who will return to society seeking to get even? John Irwin, retired sociology professor at San Francisco State University, expressed his support for that concern when he stated that "... convicts come out and they're enraged" (Morain, 1998).

The minimum goals of any correctional administrator include the desire that no one leave their custody worse off than when they entered. But one can't help being concerned about the lasting impact that programs such as forced participation in chain gangs might have on an already potentially violent offender. What will be the long-term consequences of forcing offenders to wear pink underwear and to eat food loaf for no other reason than to be punitive? Alvin Bronstein of the American Civil Liberty Union's National Prison Project expressed his concern over the "... spirit of meanness, selfishness and punitiveness that seems to have no bounds" (Gest, 1995).

How much punishment is enough and at what point is it counterproductive? This is an old question that needs a fresh look in view of the changing attitudes of America toward punishment and prisons. Criminologist Dennis J. Stevens asserts that the adage, "violence begets violence," holds true in prisons also (Stevens, 1997). In one study he found that inmates who had been subjected to less volatile prison environments expressed less interest in re-offending upon release. Harsh enforcement of rules caused more disciplinary problems and resistance to rules, rather than compliance.

There is growing concern that prisons, and particularly the new wave of punitive measures, may turn nonviolent offenders into violent offenders. Public officials should seek out the advice and counsel of experienced correctional administrators before passing legislative mandates that significantly alter prison environments. Arthur Schlesinger, Jr. once said that "Politics is about the search for remedy" (Ruff, 1993). Legislative and public officials engaged in the national debate over the toughening of our prisons need to step back and analyze

7

Legislating Barriers to Effective Solutions

An Indelicate Tool for a Complex Problem

William J. Rold

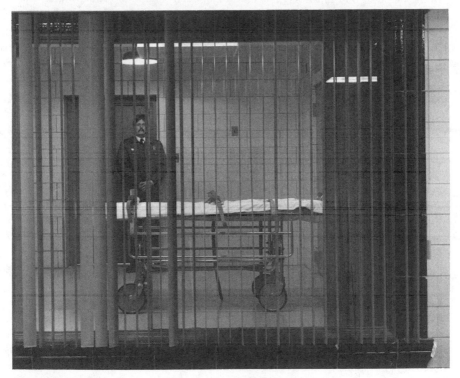

Figure 7.1 The gurney for lethal injections in Illinois.

Photograph by Lloyd DeGreen. Reprinted with permission.

[T]he more highways were built to alleviate congestion, the more automobiles would pour onto them and congest them and thus force the building of more highways—which would generate more traffic and become congested in their turn in an inexorably widening spiral that contained the most awesome implications for the future.

R. A. Caro, *The Power Broker*, p. 897

Like the urban planners who eventually saw that building more freeways would increase road congestion and reduce safety, criminologists of the 21st century will look back on the incarceration rates of the 1980s and 1990s, shake their heads, and marvel at the folly of the frenzy to incarcerate more and more people in the name of public safety. The result has been (and is) a reduction in public safety, due to the growing disrespect for and lack of confidence in the rule of law.

Current criminal justice law fosters not safer streets but more violence, as those against whom the policies are directed become more disillusioned, angrier, more cynical, and, in fact, more violent. Our increasing reliance on criminal law as a remedy of first resort for public safety issues, and the increasingly rigid application of criminal law to the detriment of judicial discretion in shaping sentencing to the circumstances of individual offenders, can build defiance and make criminal sanctions counterproductive.

Criminal Law as the Solution of First Resort

As a litigious society, America graduates more lawyers and sues more frequently than any country in the world. Rather than viewing a lawsuit as a last resort (representing a breakdown in the natural order of things, as the Confucianists saw it), we tend readily to sue as a method of grievance redress. It would likely follow, then, that policymakers turn to criminal law as the preferred solution to the problem of social disorder.

In the last decade, Congress has provided broader federal criminal jurisdiction over behaviors traditionally considered to be within the sphere of state legislation. This "federalization" of crimes has burdened the federal courts, which now spend well over half of their time hearing criminal matters. Nearly 60% of federal prisoners now committed are sentenced on criminal drug charges, an increase from approximately 10,000 inmates to more than 50,000 in ten years. This has created an overload of the system, which is to the detriment of civil cases, including the traditional function of federal courts in protecting civil rights—often the rights of the very persons they are now incarcerating in such growing numbers. These persons consequently lose confidence in their protector.

Federal conviction places the offender in the custody of the attorney general, for placement anywhere the Federal Bureau of Prisons has a facility. A convict from the Mississippi Delta may find himself imprisoned in upstate New York, or a woman from the inner city may be shipped to the Arizona desert. This federal diaspora uproots people from their communities and the support of (or even visits with) their families and friends, often creating resentment against the system. The prisoner transportation system has become so complex that the Bureau has contracted its own air fleet.

The massive increase in incarceration as a first resort also applies to the states, which house 10 times as many prisoners as the federal system. The lifetime likelihood of going to state or federal prison (not including arrest or jail) is 1 in 11 for men and 1 in 91 for women (Bonczaw & Beck, 1997). Certain populations have even higher rates, such as nearly 1 in 3 for African American men. This disparity furthers suspicion and distrust of the criminal justice system among such groups.

Much of the prison growth has been fostered by legislated American drug policy. Criminologists note that inner-city drug users are more frequently arrested because their street drug markets operate more openly than do drug transactions in middle-class areas, which usually occur in private. This disparity builds resentment because the use patterns are not as disproportionate. It is more likely that a drug addict will find himself or herself in a prison cell than in a substance abuse center, unless he or she has money, insurance, or prominence. Federal Judge Stanley Sporkin validated that concern as he testified before a congressional committee: "Recently, I was told under the sentencing guidelines, I would be required essentially to sentence a drug addict to a ten year period of incarceration. If this person were from a different socio-economic background, he would have gone to the Betty Ford Clinic for 60 to 90 days" ("Impact of Sentencing Guidelines on Federal Courts," 1997).

Communities with high incarceration rates also take note of and cast suspicion on the profiteers of incarceration. Recent corrections conventions have seen a proliferation of "for profit" enterprises providing services to institutions—or in some places actually performing the incarceration itself. In addition to converting mental hospitals and military bases to prisons, such private companies have constructed extra cells purely on speculation that they will be needed later. Prison beds are then made available to bidders from other jurisdictions, as if cells and inmates were no different than commodities, to be traded in a correctional "futures" market like soybeans or cattle. This growing industry has the potential to distort public policy decisions in criminal justice as it seeks to pursue the "profits from extended incarceration" (Schichor, 1995, p. 53). This cannot but increase the cynicism and despair of those who find themselves caught in the ever-growing correctional-industrial complex.

Restriction of Judicial Discretion

One of the oldest maxims in the law is that the wheels of justice grind slowly but they grind exceedingly fine—a recognition of an effort carefully to tailor legal dispositions to the specific circumstances of the parties before the court. Recent legislation has so restricted the options of judges, however, that the "fine" grinding of the past risks being replaced by the "meat" grinding of the future, as criminal defendants are pushed through the system at increasingly faster rates.

Consider again the testimony of Judge Sporkin ("Impact of Sentencing Guidelines on Federal Courts," 1997):

> Prior to the enactment of the Sentencing Reform Act of 1984, a convicted criminal was required to be sentenced by a judge who had to look that person in the eye and listen to what he or she had to say before imposing sentence. Based on what the defendant said, the presentence report and allocution by the prosecutor and defense counsel, sentence was pronounced. To many judges what the person said and his or her contrition were very important in imposing sentence. This is not necessarily the case any longer. Now appellate courts have gotten into the act. Where a sentence has been appealed, the appellate court becomes a new factor in what the ultimate sentence is. This is so even though the three judge panel has not seen or personally heard from the defendant. This is a clear deviation from the way our criminal justice system has operated for over 200 years. There seems to be something fundamentally wrong where our system now allows an individual to, in effect, be sentenced in absentia.

Federal and state systems continue to pass more mandatory sentences and "three strikes" legislation, establish fixed sentencing "guidelines," and eliminate parole. Each of these further erodes judicial discretion. Some in the public believe these laws have been designed to target certain communities. For example, federal drug laws that mandate mandatory minimum sentences of five years for possession of five or more grams of crack cocaine, a drug more prevalent in African American neighborhoods, permit 100 times that quantity of powder cocaine, a drug more prevalent in white neighborhoods, to be possessed before a similar sentence is imposed. As Justice Leah Sears, an African American on the Georgia Supreme Court, wrote: "When it comes to grappling with racial issues in the criminal justice system today, often white Americans find one reality while African Americans see another" (*Lingo v. State,* 1993).

Probably nowhere in criminal justice has the diminution of judicial discretion been so stark as in the application of the death penalty. The United States is one of only five nations that still allows the execution of children (the others are Iran, Pakistan, Saudi Arabia, and Yemen) (Bright, 1998, p. 34). Although we do not kill the truly insane (*Ford v. Wainwright,* 1986), since the death penalty was reinstated in 1976 at least 27 mentally retarded persons have been executed, and only 11 states prohibit this practice (Bright, 1998, p. 33).[1] In light of the fact that 70 people sentenced to death in the United States in the last 20 years have been found innocent and released from death row (Bright, 1998, p. 30), the American Bar Association's House of Delegates called for a moratorium on the death penalty in February 1997, until states could "ensure that death penalty cases are administered fairly and impartially, in accordance with due process" (Bright, 1998, p. 31).

The Supreme Court has recognized that the race of the *victim* is the most pivotal factor in determining who will be executed for homicides, but it has nevertheless sustained such disparity, writing that it is an "inevitable part of our criminal justice system" (McCleskey v. Kemp, 1987).[2] Justice William Brennan dissented from the decision, warning against the temptation to pretend that those condemned to die "share a fate in no way connected to our own; that our treatment of them sounds no echoes beyond the chamber in which they die" and reminded us that "the way in which we choose those who will die reveals the depth of our moral commitment among the living" (Bright, 1998, p. 34).

Effects of Criminal Justice Policy

People are more apt to follow laws when they agree with them and respect the legitimacy of the community and agency administering the laws (Sherman, 1993). Our reliance on criminal law as first resort and its increasingly rigid application does damage to these conditions and subsequent respect for the justice system. Perceived disparities in the construction or enforcement of the laws make compliance less likely, and, for some, provoke defiance of the law as a means of achieving solidarity with peers who also sense injustice.

Throughout the last two decades, as politicians, sometimes through demagoguery, compete to be "toughest" on crime, we have witnessed an increasingly harsh approach to social disarray, using the criminal justice system as the indelicate tool of choice for sophisticated problems. I am not a prison abolitionist. Having met thousands of inmates over the last 20 years, I can state without reservation that there are some individuals who cannot live in society without posing a danger to others and whom I would not want to see released from custody.

The cost of our present incarceration "binge," however, has been immense in terms of resources diverted from other societal goals and in the effect it has had (and is having) on respect for the rule of law. Our overreliance on incarceration threatens the fabric of our social order and our view of ourselves as a compassionate nation. The incarceration highways we are building do not make us safer, nor do they pave for our posterity a better route to rehabilitation or to relief from the surfeit of crime.

Notes

1. See, generally, K. S. Miller & M. L. Radelet (1993). *Executing the Mentally Ill.* Newbury Park, CA: Sage.

2. Finding that, of 210 people on death row in Pennsylvania, 130 were African Americans, the Pennsylvania Bar has also called for a moratorium on executions. See Bright, S. B. (1994). Counsel for the Poor: The Death Sentence Not for the Worst Crime But For the Worst Lawyer. *Yale Law Journal, 103,* p. 1835.

References

Bonczaw, T. P., & Beck, A. J. (1997). *Lifetime likelihood of going to state or federal prison* (NCJ-160092.). Washington, DC: Department of Justice, Bureau of Justice Statistics.

Bright, S. B. (1998, Summer). Death penalty moratorium: Fairness, integrity at stake. *Criminal Justice, 13, 30-34.*

Caro, R. A. (1975). *The power broker.* New York: Random House.

Ford v. Wainwright, 477 U.S. 399 (1986).

Impact of sentencing guidelines on federal courts. Testimony before the Symposium on 10th Anniversary of Sentencing Guidelines. (1997, Sept. 9). Senate Judiciary Committee, testimony of S. Sporkin. Washington, DC.

Lingo v. State, 437 S.E. 2d 463, 468 (Ga. 1993).

McCleskey v. Kemp, 481 U.S. 279 (1987).

Schichor, D. (1995). *Punishment for profit.* Thousand Oaks, CA: Sage.

Sherman, L. W. (1993). Defiance, deterrence, and irrelevance: A theory of the criminal sanction. *Journal of Research in Crime and Delinquency, 30* (4), 445-473.

8

The Racial Dynamics of Imprisonment

Marc Mauer

By the close of the 20th century, after a quarter of a century of continuously rising rates of incarceration, prisons in the United States are increasingly serving as institutions of the poor and minorities. Half of all prison inmates today are African American and 16% are Hispanic (Mumola & Beck, 1997); their median annual income prior to incarceration was less than $10,000.

It is not just the prison system, though, but the entire criminal justice system that has come to be almost a determining factor in the lives of many minorities, black men in particular. On any given day in 1995, an estimated one in three black males between 20 and 29 years of age were under some form of criminal justice supervision—either in prison or jail, or on probation or parole (Mauer & Huling, 1995). An African American boy born in 1991 faces a 3 in 10 chance of being incarcerated as an adult (Bonczar & Beck, 1997, p. 1). Although the figures for African American women are less dramatic, their rate of growth in the system has progressed at an even faster pace. From 1985 to 1995, the number of African American women incarcerated in prison or jail rose by 190%, far above the 105% increase for all other demographic groups during that same period (Bureau of Justice Statistics, 1997, p. 7).

Although these figures have come to seem almost commonplace, they represent a critical increase in a relatively short time period. In 1950, just prior to the beginning of the civil rights era, 30% of offenders admitted to prison were African Americans, a number disproportionate to their overall population. More striking, however, is the fact that by 1997 this figure had increased to nearly 50%.

The irony of these changes is that they occurred during a period of progress in many ways for minorities. Achievements of the civil rights era have led to increased economic and educational opportunities for many, and within the criminal justice system some of the most egregious forms of racism have substantially diminished. Greater opportunities, albeit limited in many ways, have emerged, so that more minority individuals have become judges, lawyers, and police chiefs. And although high profile police beatings or killings serve as reminders of the historic and continued tension between law enforcement and the African American community, the overt physical brutality exhibited by the police in the past has been significantly diminished in many cities.

Given these changes, how can we explain the rising rates of imprisonment of African Americans in recent years? Much debate has ensued over whether the racial disparities in imprisonment are the result of higher rates of crime among African American males, or of criminal justice policies that unfairly punish African American offenders.

Examining national prison data, a number of studies suggest that many of the observed disparities are related to higher rates of serious crime. Criminologist Alfred Blumstein's research concluded that 76% of the national disparities in imprisonment can be explained by higher rates of offending among African Americans (Blumstein, 1993). Other research has found that, when examining regional data, substantial variations exist within different states in the degree to which imprisonment disparities are correlated with crime rates. Studies in New York state and other jurisdictions have found that minorities are more likely to suffer unequal treatment at sentencing in misdemeanor and less serious felony cases, where greater discretion is often available to sentencing judges. This could be a result of racial bias or a combination of race and class effects in which some offenders avoid prison terms because of the resources they can mobilize—legal support, sentencing consultants, or treatment programs. The chances of entering the criminal justice system in the first place are dependent on race: African Americans are more likely to be stopped, questioned, and detained by local law enforcement agencies.

The area that illustrates the greatest disparity between offending rates and imprisonment is that of drug offenses. For drug crimes, one half of the observed disparity in imprisonment cannot be explained by the higher rates of offending cited in Blumstein's analysis. Since the beginning of the "war on drugs" in the early 1980s, there has been a qualitative shift in the focus of the criminal justice system, with profound effects for the African American community. This has come about through the combined impact of two overlapping trends: first, a dramatically accelerated pace of drug arrests and convictions, and second, a disproportionate impact of these policies on the African American community, resulting from a greater likelihood of arrest and imprisonment than whites.

During the 1980s, adult arrests for drug offenses went from fewer than 500,000 in 1980 to 1.2 million by 1989 (Federal Bureau of Investigation, 1997, p. 272). With the advent of a new generation of mandatory sentencing laws and other harsh policies, the likelihood of receiving a prison sentence for a drug arrest increased dramatically as well, rising more than fourfold from 1980 to 1992 (Beck & Gilliard, 1995, p. 13) The combined impact of these changes is reflected in the composition of correctional populations: Drug offenders were 8.6% of the state prison population in 1985, but 22.7% ten years later. The increase in federal prisons was even more dramatic, with drug offenders rising from one third of the population in 1985 to three fifths by 1995 (Bureau of Justice Statistics, 1997, pp. 10, 12).

The impact of the drug war on the African American community has had a special significance. Although government surveys show that drug use cuts across class and racial lines, law enforcement priorities have specifically concentrated resources on inner city communities where drug use and selling is more likely to be conducted in "open air" drug markets. As a result, African Americans represented 38% of all those arrested for drug offenses in 1996 and 58% of those incarcerated on drug charges in state prisons. Within the federal prison system, from 1990 to 1996, drug offenses accounted for a greater share of the increase among African American inmates (82%) than for either whites (65%) or Hispanics (67%).

The disproportionate representation of African Americans in the prison population reflects a mix of crime rates and criminal justice policies and practices. We would be remiss, however, if we were to just leave the discussion at this point without examining the assumptions underlying these dynamics.

Even to the extent that disproportionate rates of imprisonment may reflect higher rates of crime or drug abuse, it is not at all clear that enhanced use of the criminal justice system is the most effective, let alone compassionate, response possible. Looking at drug abuse, for example, a national "war on drugs" has been waged since the early 1980s, and has resulted in an enormous increase in the number of nonviolent offenders in prison. This "war," though, has concentrated its focus on drug use in minority communities, using unprecedented police and prison resources.

The problem with this strategy is that a host of evidence has documented far more effective ways of curbing drug abuse and drug-related crime than continually expanding the level of incarceration. For example, the RAND Corporation has concluded that expanding resources used for drug treatment would reduce crimes against persons 15 times more than expanding the use of mandatory minimum prison sentences (Caulkins, Rydell, Schwabe, & Chiesa, 1997).

Treatment approaches are, in fact, exactly the methods used by middle- and upper-class families who respond to a person's drug problem outside the criminal justice system. The problem is identified as a health issue and appropriate treatment resources are sought.

The large-scale imprisonment of offenders has further resulted in a diminution of political power in the African American community. As a result of state laws regarding the disenfranchisement of prisoners and ex-felons, an estimated 13% of black males are either currently or permanently disenfranchised from voting (Fellner & Mauer, 1998). This represents a bitter political irony, whereby policies are enacted that lead to the disproportionate incarceration of African American males, which in turn results in a declining ability within that community to affect those criminal justice policies in the political arena.

Although the policies enacted in the past quarter century have not necessarily been *designed* to incarcerate increasing populations of African Americans, it could have been easily foreseen that this was a likely impact. In legislative bodies, however, the far-reaching implications of legislation are rarely discussed, yielding instead to "quick fixes." If we are truly committed both to reducing crime and to achieving racial justice, an open examination of the factors behind the disproportionate incarceration of African American men and women is critical.

References

Beck, A. J., & Gilliard, D. K. (1995). *Prisoners in 1994.* Washington, DC: Bureau of Justice Statistics.

Blumstein, A. (1993). Racial disproportionality of U.S. prison populations revisited. *University of Colorado Law Review, 64,* (3), 743-760.

Bonczar, T. P., & Beck, A. J. (1997). *Lifetime likelihood of going to state or federal prison.* Washington, DC: Bureau of Justice Statistics.

Bureau of Justice Statistics. (1997). *Correctional populations in the United States, 1995.* Washington, DC: Author.

Caulkins, J. P., Rydell, C. P., Schwabe, W. L., & Chiesa, J. (1997). *Mandatory minimum drug sentences.* Santa Monica, CA: RAND.

Federal Bureau of Investigation. (1997). *Uniform crime reports 1996.* Washington, DC: Author.

Fellner, J., & Mauer, M. (1998). *Losing the vote: The impact of felony disenfranchisement.* Washington, DC: Human Rights Watch and The Sentencing Project.

Mauer, M., & Huling, T. (1995). *Young black Americans and the criminal justice system: Five years later.* Washington, DC: The Sentencing Project.

Mumola, C. J., & Beck, A. J. (1997). *Prisoners in 1996.* Washington, DC: Bureau of Justice Statistics.

9

The Care and Feeding of the Correctional-Industrial Complex

Elizabeth Alexander

Figure 9.1 Correctional goods and services are marketed to potential clients at an annual conference of the American Correctional Association. Regional and national correctional conventions with large exhibit halls have become commonplace in the industry.

Photograph by Robert Corwin, courtesy of the American Correctional Association. Reprinted with permission.

Prisons are a growth industry in this country. The unprecedented increases in the rate of incarceration in the United States since the 1980s are by now very old news. Far less study has been made of the economic and public policy side effects resulting from the massive increase in corrections spending.

The growth of the corrections industry has recently been likened to a debate of another era. In his famous speech of the 1950s, President Eisenhower sought a discussion of the extent to which American military policy was subject to distortion by what he called the "military-industrial complex." Similarly today, commentators speak of a "correctional-industrial complex" made up of private industry, governmental bureaucrats, and politicians fueling our criminal justice policy.[1]

It is stunning to recognize that the correctional-industrial complex is in fact comparable in size to its older namesake. Public expenditures for law enforcement efforts and private expenditures for security each year total $165 billion, a figure comparable to what the United States spends on the military. In 1994 alone, direct expenditures on corrections amounted to over $31 billion, an increase of 359% since 1980 (American Correctional Association, 1994, pp. 43-46).

Employment in the corrections industry is the fastest growing segment of the governmental workforce. Among *Fortune* 500 companies, only General Motors employs more people. Moreover, the greatest fiscal impact is yet to come. In 1995, governmental units spent $2 billion on prison and jail construction. The future cost of this construction is literally staggering. Each $100 million spent on prison construction commits the government to spend $1.6 billion over the following three decades in operations (Ambrosio & Schiaraldi, 1997, p. 5).

The amount of money up for grabs gives many companies and organizations a vested interest in assuring the continued expansion of the industry. The correctional officer's union in California spent more than $1 million on Governor Pete Wilson's reelection campaign. Wilson in turn has pressed for continuing expansion of California's mammoth prison system. The union went on to lobby heavily for California's "three strikes" law, which guarantees that massive increases in prison populations will continue (Donziger, 1996, p. 97).

The companies that profit from the industry are also heavy lobbyists, making hundreds of thousands of dollars in political contributions (Bloomer, 1987, p. 17). Campaign contributions, though, are but a small venue where politics and money mix, and large corporations are not the only entities that appreciate the potential for profit. In a case that exemplifies this very element, the coauthor of California's "three strikes" legislation became involved with a local campaign supporter to sell land to the California Department of Corrections for one of the new prisons that "three strikes" will require. The owner sold the land to Corrections for almost ten times its 1990 purchase price (Donziger, 1996, p. 96).

It is completely predictable that those who profit from corrections will seek to expand their industry. But this circumstance is far from the most serious consequence of the rapid growth of the correctional-industrial complex. The larger problem is that the corrections industry has taken on a social control function far expanded from its traditional primary role of incapacitating violent offenders. From 1980 to 1997, the prison and jail population in the United States more than tripled, to 1.7 million. The number of people under some form of supervision by the criminal justice system grew to more than five million, or more than 2.8% of the population (U.S. Department of Justice, 1996, p. 1). As a result, so much public capital is consumed by the industry that competing forms of public investment, particularly education, are starved.

Moreover, unlike the direct economic cost of the Cold War, the states as well as the federal government bear the costs of the "war on crime." The costs to the states have been enormous and, with little public debate or attention, those costs have resulted in a massive restructuring of state budgetary priorities. While state spending on corrections has soared, state spending on higher education has decreased by 6% since 1980. In 1995, for the first time in history, the total cost of state-issued bonds to finance prison construction surpassed the total for bonds to construct colleges (National Association of State Budget Officers, 1996, pp. 77, 98).

Budgets in California exemplify the trend. In 1980 the state spent 2.3% of its general fund expenditures on corrections, and 9.2% for higher education. By 1996, however, corrections accounted for 9.4% of the general fund, and higher education had fallen to 8.7%. Estimates from the RAND Corporation conclude that if current trends continue, in seven years California will spend 18% of its general fund on corrections (Caroll, McCarthy, & Wade, 1994). It is ironic that a state that prides itself on the amount of capital it expends on educating its residents spends so much more punishing them. The effect of the budget shifts is to decrease the subsidy for higher education, while tuition at California's colleges outpaces financial aid. For the cost of incarcerating one prisoner for a year, California could educate ten community college students, or two University of California students (Ambrosio & Schiaraldi, 1997, p. 15). While spending on University of California students primarily benefits upper-middle- and middle-class populations, spending on community college students tends to spread the subsidy across the population.

Spending to incarcerate, however, creates a fundamentally different range of economic distribution and impact. While the workers and management in corrections gain economic benefits, the communities that produce the prisoners feel a negative economic impact. Communities are not equally at risk to lose a member to incarceration. For example, 80% of those confined at Riker's Island come from seven New York City neighborhoods (Clear, 1996, p. 11). Arrests as well as convictions damage earning potential. The children and partners of the incarcerated suffer financial losses and disruptions. Imprisonment becomes a common and unremarkable part of the life experiences of the young men in a community. This produces an environment so distinct and disruptive that the community a prisoner goes to when released is a good predictor of the likelihood of the person being rearrested (Gottfredson & Taylor, 1986).

In short, one distinction between the economic effects of the correctional-industrial complex versus the military-industrial complex is that the "product" of this new complex is prisoners, and that the "process of production" serves to damage communities. While some of these offenders have also damaged their communities to various degrees, 84% of the increase in incarceration since 1980 has involved nonviolent offenders. The communities that have seen their young people, and particularly their young men, imprisoned in escalating numbers since 1980 are the same communities that have lost out economically in the last 20 years as the disparities in wealth and job training have grown substantially. Many of these communities consist of minority populations. Thus the growth in the prison industry exacerbates the chasm between the rich and the poor, and the chasm between the races. Such collateral effects of incarceration are of great cost to our country. Furthermore, the rise in felony convictions palpably reduces the percentage of eligible African American voters in the population (Donziger, 1996, pp. 127-128). The unemployment rate in the United States would appear significantly worse in comparison to other industrialized countries were it not lowered by the uniquely large percentage of the U.S. population in prison. Prison populations have become an important demographic feature of the country.

One of the most destructive side effects of the growth in the correctional-industrial complex is the extent to which it reinforces economic and social segregation and isolation of various communities in the United States. While the correctional-industrial complex lacks the destructive potential of its predecessor, this "war on crime" is not without its profiteers or its victims.

Note

1. See, e.g., Donziger, 1996, pp. 85-98; Thomas, P. (1994, May 12), Triangle of interests creates infrastructure to fight lawlessness, *The Wall Street Journal*, p. Al; and Elvin, J. (1994/95 ,Winter), "Corrections-industrial complex" expands in U.S., *The National Prison Project Journal*, 10(1), 1-3.

References

Ambrosio, T.-J., & Schiaraldi, V. (1997). *From classrooms to cell block: A national perspective.* Washington, DC: The Justice Policy Institute.

American Correctional Association. (1994). *Vital statistics in corrections.* Laurel, MD: Author.

Bloomer, K. (1987, March 17). America's newest growth industry. *In These Times,* pp. 14-18.

Caroll, S. J., McCarthy, K. F., & Wade, M. (1994). California's looming budget crisis. (Special issue.) *Rand Research Review, 18*(2).

Clear, T. R. (1996). Backfire when incarceration increases crime. In *The unintended consequences of incarceration* (pp. 1-20). New York: Vera Institute of Justice.

Donziger, S. R. (Ed.). (1996). *The real war on crime.* New York: Harper.

Gottfredson, S. D., & Taylor, R. B. (1986). Person-environment interactions in the prediction of recidivism. In R. Sampson & J. Byrne (Eds.), *Criminal social ecology.* New York: Springer-Verlag.

National Association of State Budget Officers (NASBO). (1996). *1995 state expenditures report.* Washington, DC: Author.

U.S. Department of Justice, Bureau of Justice Statistics. (1996). *Probation and parole populations: 1995.* Washington, DC: Government Printing Office.

10

Examining "Justice" in the Juvenile System

Mark Soler

The juvenile justice system has long been beset by a myriad of difficulties. The first juvenile court was established in Chicago in 1899 to provide individualized treatment and services for troubled children. There was popular support for its focus and ideals (Mack, 1909). However, at the time, the needed financial support and other resources to turn those ideals into reality did not exist.

Historically, judges, prosecutors, defenders, and probation personnel were often inexperienced, poorly trained, and unprepared to handle difficult children and families. Many jurisdictions had no social workers, medical or mental health professionals, or other experts to assist them with their responsibilities. Furthermore, community programs for troubled youth were often limited or nonexistent. Informal proceedings were supposed to facilitate concerned guidance and supervision by the juvenile court *in loco parentis,* but the *Gault* case (1967) demonstrated that those proceedings could also be arbitrary, punitive, and virtually lawless.

Following *Gault,* the pendulum swung in the opposite direction, and an adversarial system modeled on adult criminal courts was created. It has, however, been riddled with inadequacies and has hardly been a solution (Feld, 1980, 1988). Today, the juvenile justice system receives criticism from many fields: some admonish it for being too "soft" on serious youth crime, some for being too "hard" on nonviolent youth who do not require incarceration, and others for a process that fails to deliver thoughtful individualized justice.

What is clear is that once they are in the system, young people too often encounter serious problems that have little to do with the charges against them, including inexperienced and inadequate counsel, unduly harsh confinement, and racial discrimination. These difficulties challenge the notion that they can find "justice" within the juvenile justice system.

Access to Counsel and
Quality of Representation

Critical problems for youth in the juvenile justice system often begin long before incarceration. In 1995, the American Bar Association Juvenile Justice Center, with support from the Youth Law Center and the Juvenile Law Center, published the first national assessment of access to counsel and quality of representation in juvenile court (Puritz, Burrell, Schwartz, Soler, & Warboys, 1995). The study was based on questionnaires mailed to public defenders and other defense counsel in every state, as well as on-site visits to a number of juvenile courts around the country.

The results were deeply disturbing. Although the researchers found attorneys who represented their young clients with energy, commitment, and skill, this type of representation was not the norm. Not surprisingly, the enormous caseloads were the most critical problem: The average caseloads of public defenders, who represent the great majority of youth in the system, often exceed 500 cases a year, with more than 300 of those being juvenile. Regardless of an attorney's commitment or ability, high caseloads have an adverse effect on virtually every aspect of representation. Attorneys with heavy caseloads face a number of difficulties, including meeting with their clients before court to explain proceedings, conducting thorough investigations of alleged offenses, learning about the youths' families and ties to community, preparing individualized pretrial motions, keeping informed about community-based programs as alternatives to secure detention, and following up after disposition to monitor their clients' progress after placement. Further, high caseloads have a debilitating and direct impact on defense attorneys. Many either burn out or transfer out of juvenile court as quickly as they can, often resulting in the handling of these types of cases by less experienced attorneys.

Conditions of Confinement

For many youth, confinement—the end of this conveyor belt-like process—is only the beginning of their problems. Each year more than 300,000 youth are incarcerated in local juvenile detention facilities prior to adjudication in juvenile court, and more than 65,000 are admitted to state institutions as a consequence of adjudication and disposition. In addition, more than 65,000 are confined in adult jails for some period of time or held briefly in police stations and sheriff's substations (Snyder & Sickmund, 1995; Snyder, Sickmund, & Poe-Yamagata, 1997).

In 1994 the Office of Juvenile Justice and Delinquency Prevention published the first national study of conditions of juvenile confinement (Parent et al., 1994). The study, conducted by Abt Associates, consisted of a written survey to the 984 juvenile facilities in the United States, as well as site visits to 95 of those facilities.

The study found substantial deficiencies and dangerous conditions. First, over half the incarcerated juvenile population is housed in overcrowded facilities. This fact profoundly affects institutional operations and inmate behavior. As a result of overcrowding, it is difficult to maintain a classification system that separates vulnerable juveniles from predatory ones; medical and mental health services are stretched so far that they can deal only with immediate crises; education programs may be cut; exercise time is reduced; sanitation becomes a much more serious problem; there is a greater chance that disruptive juveniles will be controlled with restraints, isolation, or both; and fights, assaults, and other violent acts can become a common occurrence (Lerner, 1986).

The study further found serious problems in institutional security and safety. Many facilities have inadequate staff-to-youth ratios (perhaps as high as 1:30), resulting in increased injuries, escapes, and suicide attempts. For example, in the 30 days prior to the written survey, some 2,000 youth and 650 staff were injured in juvenile facilities across the country. During that same time period, over 800 juveniles escaped from locked facilities, while more than 800 others were unsuccessful in their attempts. Additionally, in those 30 days, 970 youth committed over 1,400 reported acts of suicidal behavior—annualized, this figure represents 11,000 youth committing 17,000 suicidal acts each year.

Other reports found that the use of restraints and isolation were areas with high potential for abuse. Anecdotal reports and civil rights cases have documented extraordinarily punitive practices: youth locked in tiny, dirty rooms for days and even weeks at a time, without a hearing on any alleged misconduct; gassed with Mace or pepper spray for not coming out of their rooms when told to do so; tied by their wrists and ankles to the four corners of their beds for disobeying orders of custodial staff; and stripped to their underwear, put in four-point restraints, and injected with psychotropic drugs as "treatment" for suicidal behavior (*Hollingsworth v. Orange County,* 1990; Human Rights Watch, 1996; *Robert K. v. Bell,* 1984).

The problems are worse for youth with mental health disorders. Many juvenile facilities have been found to have inadequate professional staff or other resources to manage such individuals. Although estimates of the prevalence of specific disorders vary considerably, at least 20% and as many as 60% have conduct disorders, between 1% and 6% have psychotic disorders, a significant number have attention deficit disorders and affective disorders, many have substance abuse problems, and there is a high degree of comorbidity between mental disorders and substance abuse disorders (Otto, Greenstein, Johnson, & Friedman, 1992). Failure to meet those needs (or, worse, responding to them with punitive measures) can increase violent and disruptive behavior by confined youth. Facilities often do no more than confine them in isolation rooms, away from staff and other youth, until they are released or sent to another institution (Schwartz, 1991).

Education is another major area of concern, particularly for youth with educational disabilities. Studies estimate the prevalence of handicapping conditions from nearly 30% to over 60% of youth in the system (Murphy, 1986). Yet few facilities have adequate special education programs that meet federal or state requirements. Additionally, many of these youth suffer from undiagnosed or untreated conditions such as attention-deficit hyperactivity disorder. Such conditions are particularly problematic in confined and strictly regimented settings, where the symptoms of the disorder may often be misinterpreted by custodial staff as behavioral problems, and lead to much more restrictive control.

Racial Disparities in the System

It is important to remember who is actually in the juvenile justice system.

A multitude of research indicates that minority youth are overrepresented at every stage of the system, from arrest to incarceration after disposition (Leonard, Pope, & Feyerherm, 1995). For example, although African American youth aged 10 to 17 constitute 15% of the total population of the United States, they make up 26% of juvenile arrests, 32% of delinquency referrals to juvenile court, 41% of juveniles detained in delinquency cases, 46% of juveniles in correctional institutions, and 52% of juveniles transferred to adult criminal court after judicial hearings. In 1991, the public long-term custody rate for African American youth was nearly five times the rate for white youth (Snyder & Sickmund, 1995).

But African Americans are not the only juveniles disproportionately affected by the juvenile justice system. The number of minority youth held in detention centers increased 79% from 1983 to 1991, while the number of white youth increased by only 8%. Indeed, in a one-day census of all juvenile detention centers, minorities made up two thirds of all detained youth (Snyder & Sickmund, 1995). This is *not* due to different offense rates by white and minority youth: A study of the juvenile justice system in California found that minority youth, particularly African Americans, consistently receive more severe dispositions than white youth and are more likely to be committed to state institutions than white youth for the same offenses (Jones & Krisberg, 1994).

Conclusion

Inadequate representation, dangerous conditions of confinement, and racial disparities are the real "three strikes" in the juvenile justice system, leading to bitterness, resentment, and increased violence rather than rehabilitation, maturity, and development of a sense of responsibility. Until we make progress in these areas, violence in the system is likely to continue.

References

Feld, B. (1980). Juvenile court legislative reform and the serious young offender: Dismantling the "rehabilitative ideal." *Minnesota Law Review, 65,* 167.

Feld, B. (1988). The juvenile court meets the principle of offense: Punishment, treatment, and the difference it makes. *Boston University Law Review, 68,* 821-915.

Hollingsworth v. Orange County, No. 51-08-65 (Super. Ct. Orange Co., Calif. 1990).

Human Rights Watch. (1996). *Modern capital of human rights? Abuses in the state of Georgia.* New York: Author.

Jones, M. A., & Krisberg, B. (1994). *Images and reality: Juvenile crime, youth violence and public policy* (pamphlet). San Francisco: National Council on Crime and Delinquency.

In re Gault, 387 U.S. 1 (1967).

Leonard, K. K., Pope, C. E., & Feyerherm, W. H. (Eds.). (1995). *Minorities in juvenile justice.* Thousand Oaks, CA: Sage.

Lerner, S. (1986). *The CYA report, part two—Bodily harm: The pattern of fear and violence at the California Youth Authority.* Bolinas, CA: Commonweal Research Institute.

Mack, J. (1909).The juvenile court. *Harvard Law Review, 23,* 104.

Murphy, D. M. (1986). The prevalence of handicapping conditions among juvenile delinquents. *Remedial and Special Education, 7,* 7-17.

Otto, R., Greenstein, J., Johnson, M., & Friedman, R. (1992). Prevalence of mental disorders among youth in the juvenile justice system. In J. Cocozza (Ed.), *Responding to the mental health needs of youth in the juvenile justice system.* Seattle, WA: The National Coalition for the Mentally Ill in the Criminal Justice System.

Parent, D. G., Leiter, V., Kennedy, S., Livens, L., Wentworth, D., & Wilcox, S. (1994). *Conditions of confinement: Juvenile detention and corrections facilities.* Washington, DC: Office of Juvenile Justice and Delinquency Prevention.

Puritz, P., Burrell, S., Schwartz, R., Soler, M., & Warboys, L. (1995). *A call for justice: An assessment of access to counsel and quality of representation in delinquency proceedings.* Washington, DC: American Bar Association, Youth Law Center, and Juvenile Law Center.

Robert K. v. Bell (1984). Civil Action No. 83-287-0 (D.S.C.).

Schwartz, D. J. (1991). The three R's of mental health assessment of the forgotten child: Reluctance, resistance, and rejection. In L. Thompson (Ed.), *The forgotten child in* health care: Children in the juvenile justice system.* Washington, DC: National Center for Education in Maternal and Child Health.

Snyder, H., & Sickmund, M. (1995). *Juvenile offenders and victims: A national report.* Washington, DC: Office of Juvenile Justice and Delinquency Prevention.

Snyder, H., Sickmund, M., & Poe-Yamagata, E. (1997). *Juvenile offenders and victims: 1997 update on violence.* Washington, DC: Office of Juvenile Justice and Delinquency Prevention.

11

Adult Abdication
The Misrepresentation
of Juvenile Crime

Bernardine Dohrn

It is a bitter irony that children have become our greatest fear. At the end of a century soaked in the bloodshed of wars, genocides, ethnic and tribal slaughter, and technological assaults on civilian populations—a century whose last decade saw children become the primary victims of war[1]—we in the United States seem to have turned on our own children as the greatest threat to our security and peace. Children have become the primary targets of official "wars": the war on drugs, the war on crime, the war on gangs. Polls indicate that Americans most fear juvenile crime, and politicians have discovered that there are almost no bounds to punishment possibilities: expulsion from school, an end to confidentiality for youth offenses, boot camps, whipping, humiliation, unpaid labor, trial and sentencing as adults, incarceration of children with adult criminals, isolation and sensory deprivation, and legal executions of children.

For professionals who labor in the once invisible fields of juvenile justice —the probation officers, detention and correction workers, judges, lawyers, and youth workers—the skewed reporting of violent youth crime on nightly local TV news as a live, episodic event has created a distorted perception of most youthful offending, the possibilities for youth recovery, and the work of juvenile courts.

Media Distortions

In a recent study of TV news coverage in 56 cities, crime stories made up one third of all news (Klite, Bardwell, & Salzman, 1997). In Los Angeles, there is an average of three reports of crime during the 30-minute local newscast, accounting for a full four minutes of twelve devoted to "news" (Gilliam & Iyengar, in press). This intensive coverage of crime is further distorted by its focus on violent crime. In Los Angeles, murder stories were 30% of crime coverage, although murders represent some 2% of *felony* crime and a lesser percent of all crime (Gilliam & Iyengar, in press). Furthermore, this extensive media depiction of violent crime has become a concentration on violent youth crime (Berry & Manning-Miller, 1996; Males, 1996).

Youth are commonly portrayed as remorseless (Drizin, 1998, p. 15)[2], cold-hearted, and amoral; as a virulent disease (plague, pestilence, scourge, cancer, virus, blight, desease, infestation, parasitic) (Conquergood, 1997, pp. 1-2); as vicious animals (roving wolfpack, beasts of prey, vermin) (Conquergood, 1997, pp. 2-3); or violent terrorists (barbarians, savages, guerrillas, killing machines, incendiary bombs) (Conquergood, 1997, pp. 3-4). This dehumanizing and de-contextualized language, used daily to characterize adolescent American children in our contemporary "heart of darkness," would never be publicly tolerated today if used to describe racial, ethnic, or religious groups. It is, however, part of a pervasive and powerful news icon: the child superpredator (Squires & Etteman, 1997, p. 104).[3] The icon is part of an overall framing, which identifies problems, defines causes, makes moral judgments, and suggests remedies (Entman, 1993). The surge in reporting youth crime between 1992 and 1995 produced more frequent recommendations for increased punitive penalties, while remedies calling for prevention or intervention sharply declined (Squires & Ettema, 1997). The impact of this distorted and saturated news coverage of youth crime includes popular uncritical acceptance of the notion of a coming wave of predator children, a circumscribed political discussion on feasible approaches to youth crime, and politicians promoting punitive solutions which have been made more palatable.

Facts on youth crime frequently seem irrelevant. Analysis of both national and local data illustrates some dramatic realities which conflict with dominant popular and political perception.

Basic Youth Crime Realities

- 95% of all youth are never arrested. Of the 5% who are arrested, 94% are arrested for nonviolent offenses (Snyder & Sickmund, 1995, p. 51).[4]

- Most juveniles coming into contact with the juvenile justice system do so only once (Snyder & Sickmund, 1995, pp. 49-50).

- Less than one half of 1% of youth between 10 and 17 years old were charged with a serious, violent offense as defined by the U.S. Department of Justice violent crime index in 1992 (Snyder & Sickmund, 1995, p. 51).

- Of the 500,000 children incarcerated for delinquency or crime, the vast majority are locked up for nonviolent offenses. Studies indicate that less than 14% of juveniles committed to correctional institutions were sentenced for the most serious, violent offenses. The majority are confined for property and drug offenses (Jones & Krisberg, 1994, pp. 27-28). A recent U.S. Department of Justice report on juvenile prisons in Georgia found "egregious," "abusive," and "grossly substandard" conditions for the 25,000 young inmates. Three quarters of these young people were incarcerated for a nonviolent offense; one third of the children were locked up merely for being status offenders (Butterfield, 1998).

If the above facts fly in the face of what is regularly heard, what is accurate about our national preoccupation with youth crime? Criminologists agree that there was indeed a particular youth crime epidemic in the decade 1984-1994: the dramatic and tragic spiking of youth homicide. The monumental reality of children killing children—while a tiny portion of delinquency cases or even of youth violence—is defining policy that affects all youth, all youthful offenders, and all crime.

Children Killing Children

Youth homicide reached epidemic proportions between 1984 and 1994, increasing 160% for 14- to 17-year-old offenders (Snyder & Sickmund, 1995, p. 56). The impact of this carnage is disproportionate: The number one cause of death for African American boys between the ages of 15 and 24 is murder. For each child who is killed, at least two are wounded by gunfire and survive. Thousands more are witnesses, neighbors, classmates, or family members of the children who kill or are killed.

The instrument propelling the *lethal* epidemic of children killing children is firearms. During the decade when youth homicide by guns quadrupled, non-gun youth homicide rates remained flat. Almost 80% of youth homicides were committed with firearms in 1991 (Lotke & Schiraldi, 1996, p. 7). America's children are killed by guns at 12 times the rate of children in the other 25 industrialized nations combined. Youth homicide is remarkably site-specific, concentrated in a handful of urban areas. Six states make up more than half the youth homicide arrests; four cities (Los Angeles, New York, Chicago, and Detroit) account for one third of the arrests. Fully 93.4% of counties in the United States experienced one or no juvenile homicides in 1995 (Lotke and Schiraldi, 1996, p. 3).

What has changed is not the nature of children, nor their numbers, but that fighting and violence among adolescent males has become *lethal* violence (Canada, 1995). Youth fighting, gang retaliation, and adolescents' need for respect become fatal with the easy availability of handguns to children (Zimring and Hawkins, 1997). Sixty-five percent of high schoolers indicate that it would be easy for them to get a gun.

Good News/Bad News

The hopeful conclusion behind the data is that most adolescents in trouble with the law can recover, acknowledge the consequences of their actions, and move on to become productive and creative citizens (Schulhofer, 1997).[5] Children respond to how they are treated; they watch what adults do and fail to do. The Boston Cease-Fire Task Force achieved dramatic impact by creating conditions for Boston youth which resulted in two years without a single youth homicide (Butterfield, 1996; Kennedy, 1997). A coordinated approach to stopping the shooting and the killing can succeed. Interrupting the easy access of handguns for children is possible with sustained adult action. Tackling our social priorities—so that it becomes intolerable for one fourth of the children in the wealthiest nation in the world to be born into poverty—is a fully human determination, and readily attainable.[6]

It is clear that a practical and effective approach to youth crime would contain several elements: first, a concentrated and coordinated approach to reducing and sustaining a drastically reduced level of youth homicides and shootings. This end to the urban killing fields and the fear of gunfire itself brings back community activity, adult presence, and cooperative efforts. A second element would be sustained efforts to keep kids in school, not expelling them unless all other resources and efforts have been exhausted. All evidence shows that school attendance is a major predictor of whether children are arrested. We can develop appropriate school guidelines yet be flexible about youth behavior, so mistakes by youth become a teaching opportunity and not an occasion for punishment, exile, and failure. Children can get involved in conflict resolution in teen courts, peer mediation, and mentoring. Third, create jobs and training and placement opportunities to move youth toward a productive working future. Fourth, develop community justice initiatives to hold children accountable for youthful offending in ways that repair the harm to victims, family, and neighborhood. Fifth, create neighborhood alternatives to costly and failing incarceration policies, such as evening reporting centers, citizen youth mediation panels, and family support centers. Finally, advocate for what *all* children need to have a hopeful future.

Notes

1. *The State of the World's Children 1996.* (1996). UNICEF: Oxford University Press, p. 13. During the past decade, it is estimated that 2 million children have been killed, 4-5 million disabled, 12 million made homeless, more than 1 million orphaned, and some 10 million traumatized by warfare.

2. News stories that depicted child offenders as remorseless jumped from 25% in 1993 to 67% in 1994 in one study (Squires & Ettema, 1997).

3. The phrase "superpredator" was popularized by Princeton criminologist John DiIulio, Jr., who refers to youth as "fatherless, godless and jobless" and promoted by James Q. Wilson, public policy professor at UCLA, who describes young offenders who "show us the blank, unremorseful stare of a feral, presocial being." Quoted in F. Zimring, "Crying Wolf Over Teen Demons," *Los Angeles Times*, August 19, 1996, p. B-6.

4. See also Sickmund, M., Snyder, H. N., & Poe-Yamagata, E. (1997). *Juvenile Offenders and Victims: 1997 Update on Violence: Statistics Summary.* Washington, DC: National Center for Juvenile Justice.

5. See, e.g., Hawkins, D. & Catalano, R., Jr. (1992). *Communities that care.* San Francisco: Jossey-Bass; Greenwood, P., et al. (1996). *Diverting children from a life of crime: Measuring costs and benefits.* Santa Monica, CA: RAND; Wilson, J. J., & Howell, J. C. (1993). *A comprehensive strategy for serious, violent and chronic juvenile offenders.* Washington, DC: Office of Juvenile Justice and Delinquency Prevention, U.S. Department of Justice.

6. "Children and Poverty." (1997, Summer/Fall). In *The Future of Children*, 7(2). Center for the Future of Children, The David and Lucile Packard Foundation; "State Profiles of Child Well-Being." (1997). In *Kids Count Data Book* 1997. Baltimore, MD: The Annie E. Casey Foundation; *The State of America's Children Yearbook 1998.* (1998). Washington, DC: Children's Defense Fund.

References

Berry, V., & Manning-Miller, C. (1996). *Mediated messages and African-American culture.* Thousand Oaks, CA: Sage.

Butterfield, F. (1996, Nov. 21). In Boston, nothing is something. *The New York Times*, p. A8.

Butterfield, F. (1998, March 22). U.S. and Georgia deal to improve juvenile prison. *The New York Times*, section 1, p. 16.

Canada, G. (1995). *Fist, stick, knife, glove.* Boston: Beacon.

Conquergood, D. (1997). *The power of symbols.* A report to the Human Relations Foundation of Chicago. Northwestern University.

Drizin, S. A. (1998, April 27). Should we demand juveniles to cry us a river? *Chicago Tribune*, sect. 1, p. 15.

Entman, R. (1993). Framing: Toward clarification of a fractured paradigm. *Journal of Communication*, 51-58.

Gilliam, F. D., Jr., & Iyengar, S. (In press). Super-predators or wayward youth? Framing effects in crime news coverage. In N. Terkildsen & F. Schnell (Eds.), *The dynamics of issue framing: Elite discourse and the formation of public opinion.* New York: Cambridge University Press.

Jones, M. A., & Krisberg, B. (1994). *Images and reality: Juvenile crime, youth violence and public policy.* San Francisco: National Council on Crime and Delinquency.

Kennedy, D. M. (1997, March). Juvenile gun violence and gun markets in Boston. *National Institute of Justice Research Preview.*

Klite, P., Bardwell, R., & Salzman J. (1997). Local television news: Getting away with murder. *Harvard International Journal of Press/Politics, 2*, 102-112.

Lotke, E., & Schiraldi, V. (1996). *An analysis of juvenile homicides: Where they occur and the effectiveness of adult court intervention,* p. 7. Alexandria, VA: National Center on Institutions and Alternatives, Center on Juvenile and Criminal Justice.

Males, M. (1996). *The scapegoat generation: America's war on adolescents.* Monroe, ME: Common Courage Press.

Schulhofer, S. J. (1997). Guns and violence—Youth crime and what not to do about it. *Valparaiso University Law Review, 31*(2), 435.

Snyder, H. N., & Sickmund, M. (1995). *Juvenile offenders and victims: A national report.* Washington, DC: Office of Juvenile Justice and Delinquency Prevention, U.S. Department of Justice.

Squires, C. R., & Ettema, J. S. (1997, February). Superpredators in the news and public policy. Report to the Human Relations Foundation of Chicago.

Zimring, F. E., Hawkins, G. (1997). *Crime is not the problem: Lethal violence in America.* New York: Oxford Uniersity Press.

Part III

Casualties of
Mass Incarceration

The growth in prison populations has drawn disproportionately from many groups, including persons of color, the mentally ill, children, the poor, and immigrants. Drug users, the terminally ill, and the elderly are subjected to the same conditions as malicious offenders. Prisons do not easily accommodate changing populations, so those with the least power must struggle with what is dealt them. The following chapters speak to the policies and consequences of incarcerating certain populations.

12

The Politics of Jailing

Juan Williams

Figure 12.1 Working like an assembly line, jails and prisons in the United States process more than 10 million people each year. This is the reception center for the Illinois Department of Corrections.

Photograph by Lloyd DeGreen. Reprinted with permission.

Jails and political oppression often go hand in hand.

Recent history is all too clear on this point. A corrupt, strong-armed Nigerian military jailed Moshood Abiola, the man who won a free election to become the leader of his nation. The military wanted him under control. Similarly, a brutal, authoritarian regime jailed Alexander Solzhenitsyn, the Russian dissident and 1970 Nobel Peace Prize winner, when his writings opened a window on his nation's brutal regime. Nelson Mandela, another Nobel Peace Prize recipient, spent 27 years in jail for his attempt to beat back the political and military might of South Africa's apartheid regime.

Closer to home, racist southern sheriffs jailed Martin Luther King, Jr., also a Nobel winner, to intimidate—and stop—King's marches against government-enforced racial segregation. One of King's most famous writings is his Letter from a Birmingham Jail (King, 1986).

In the rapid growth of America's prison system today a new twist has been added to the abuse of jail. Imprisoning large numbers of people is now a profitable business. The prisons in the United States increasingly warehouse people who are unwanted in society—the poor, racial minorities, the ill-educated, and the mentally ill. Poor quality public schools and a shrinking blue collar economy are forcing more people to the margins of American life and the status of undesirables. Those lost souls find their only productive social role is as fodder for the ever-growing number of jails. And blacks and Hispanics—disproportionately poor—are being disproportionately jailed in shocking numbers.

But fear of criminal behavior by the underemployed and ill-educated has altered public opinion (specifically white public opinion) to the point that, even as crime rates decrease nationwide, there is strong support for putting more and more people in jail. This political pressure has led to requiring jail sentences for possession of even minuscule amounts of drugs. In the past few years, longer prison sentences and even life sentences, notably for repeat offenders under the "three strikes" rule, has become an accepted part of America's national crime policy.

The combination of politically-driven fantasies about criminals running rampant in the streets and a widening economic and social divide between rich and poor has led the nation to a moral blindness about the consequences of mass jailing. Even more chilling is the growth of a prison industry that is viewed as an economic tonic for depressed rural areas of the country—a source of construction jobs, employment for jail guards, and contracts for every local business from food services to plumbers.

This increase in American prisoners can be seen most starkly in the increase in black people in the jails. Adding to the friction, prisons are cropping up in areas with predominantly white, working class populations, and racial antagonisms quickly emerge between the people in the jail and the people gaining economic benefit from the jail.

This criminalization of a large percentage of the nation's black population creates staggering social realities, which illustrate the damage done by the current embrace of putting large segments of the population in prison. Putting men in jail damages families by taking away not only potential wage earners, but also fathers, sons, brothers, husbands, and boyfriends. For example, half of the young black men in Washington, D.C. between the ages of 18 and 35 are in jail, under court supervision, or wanted by the police. The situation in Washington is not very different than in most U.S. cities—it's just that Washington has a very high percentage of blacks in its population.

On a psychological level there are consequences, too. The idea of "throw-away" people—humans who are deficient, weak, or criminal—is a sharp departure from the idea of jails as a place to punish but also reform and rehabilitate people who have taken a wrong turn. America has accepted, with its ever-growing prison population, the idea of real-life, human monsters who are beyond redemption. The only "reforms" are the death penalty, now more popular than ever, or caging the monsters away from decent people for life. And if the decision is made to give a life sentence, American popular opinion now is to make that lifetime in jail as debilitating as possible. There are movements nationwide to remove exercise equipment, libraries, and educational facilities from jails on the theory that people who commit crimes should not benefit from their time in jail. In the current mind-set, jails are solely for punishment.

Young black people are being bombarded with images of themselves that equate being black with criminal life. Black identity in American song, movies, and fashion is not about intellectual achievement, romance, or artistic triumph. Instead, visions of gangster rappers, drive-by shootings, alienated black boys, and jailhouse fashions (pants without belts hanging off hips) are offered as the quintessence of black identity and culture. It is bad enough that this message is sent to white America, as it exacerbates negative stereotypes of black people as criminal and violent. The worst impact, however, is specifically on black children, who come to see themselves and every other black person as absent of any future except that of inmate for the ever-growing prison industry.

In historical terms, these awful realities rival psychologist Ken Clark's findings in the 1940s and 1950s that black children were being taught self-hate as a result of segregation (Clark, 1963). Today that self-hate, the sense of black people as different and inferior to other citizens, attaches to the idea of blacks as criminals and convicts. At essence, this is society stamping people as being unworthy, not to be trusted, and lacking in diligence and intellect. Polls show that these negative stereotypes all fit with the preconceptions of many white Americans.

The double-edged sword in any argument against prison expansion is that there is an indisputably real fear of crime. This fear is especially true in black neighborhoods. While crime rates are falling nationally, violent crime is slightly increasing, and usually in areas where unemployment and drug abuse have a firm and deadly grip. Most often the victims of black criminals are black people.

Ironically, polls universally show that black Americans tend to be very conservative when it comes to punishing criminals, favoring long sentences and even the death penalty. Neither blacks nor whites want dangerous, predatory types, of any race, on the streets. Any argument against the warehousing of large numbers of black people in American jails is inevitably rebutted by the fact that there is a disproportionate share of criminal behavior among black people.

Given the much higher levels of broken homes, poor schools, and poverty in black and Hispanic communities, a higher incidence of crime can't be categorized as a surprise. And it can't be denied by people concerned about the high rate of incarceration of black Americans. Even so, low socioeconomic status is not an excuse and no one is arguing that crime should be ignored. The alternative to putting more and more people in jail is not excusing criminal behavior.

But just as surely as criminal behavior must be punished, jails must be reserved for criminals who are an actual threat to society. They should not be used as society's cure-all for all misfits, including people with psychological problems, the poorly educated, or drug dealers and addicts. Many of the people now being rushed to jail are not guilty of committing violent crimes. A large portion of prisoners are people convicted for drug use and sales, especially involving crack cocaine. And the increase in inmates also comes from judges forced to handle more juvenile offenders as adults under strict sentencing codes. That last policy, in combination with three strikes rules requiring life sentences for anyone with three felony convictions, can take all discretion out of the hands of judges. They have no choice but to send the people before them to jail for life.

The expanding prison industry is not an idle bystander in this conversation. Prison guards and construction contractors have created a political interest group in many states, whose sole purpose is to pressure state legislators to increase the budget for building prisons and to get tough on crime. There is no interest group pushing from the other side of this argument. In fact, the politicians are predisposed to building more jails because they have often played on the fear of violent crime in their election campaigns by promising to be tougher than the next politician. In addition, the young don't vote. Both the black and Hispanic populations in the United States are younger than the white population and have a lower rate of campaign contributions and voting. Consequently, there is little restraint on the savage appetite for putting young men, especially those of color, into the latest high-tech prisons until they are filled and the cry goes up for more prison construction.

The only brake on this savage cycle is individual conscience. It is immoral to consign so many people, fellow human souls, to such a horrible fate. On the national level, it is a corruption of American society to allow so many young people of color to become sacrificial lambs, born for a trip to the slaughterhouse of society, the modern jail. There is a high social cost—in increased racism, broken families, distorted lives, and ironically, increased violence. This is America's great tragedy at the end of the 20th century.

In all social movements the first spark has been an increased awareness of the problem. That spark starts a fire of speeches and marches until action is taken. That is the heart of American history. There was the revolutionary response to British colonialism. And there was the slow burn of defiance against Jim Crow segregation that led to the powerful eruption of the American civil rights movement in the 1950s and 1960s.

Today politicians and the media purposely turn a blind eye—and indifferent spirit—to the social damage done by a prison system with a monstrous appetite and no sense of its original mission of reforming criminal behavior. But as eyes open to the reality that the prison industry feeds on lives, the seeds of social revolution are taking root. The start of another social movement is boiling in the cauldron of this terrible social wrong.

References

Clark, K. B. (1963). *Prejudice and your child.* Boston: Beacon.

King, M. L., Jr. (1986). Letter from a Birmingham jail. In J. M. Washington (Ed.), *I have a dream: Writings and speeches that changed the world* (pp. 83-100). San Francisco: HarperSanFrancisco.

13

Inappropriate Prison Populations

B. Jaye Anno

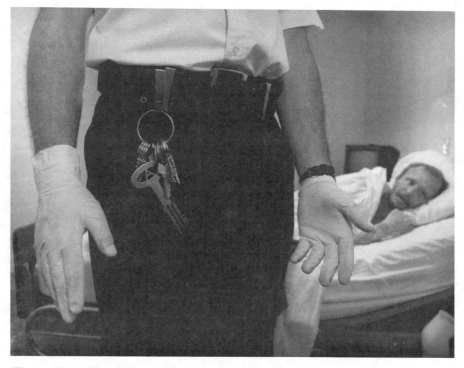

Figure 13.1 A dying inmate/patient in the prison infirmary.
Photograph by Lloyd DeGreen. Reprinted with permission.

At first glance, one may question what women, the elderly, the poor, and the terminally ill have in common. The answer is that they are linked by shared circumstance in that growing numbers of each group are being confined in our nation's prisons. Further, their commonality lies in the fact that most of them are in far greater need of social services, such as drug treatment programs, medical care, or hospice care than they are in need of isolation and punishment.

According to von Hirsch (1976), the penological literature usually lists three utilitarian aims of punishment—deterrence, incapacitation, and rehabilitation—along with a fourth aim of retribution, or, what he prefers to call "deserts." The argument can be made that the abandonment of the "rehabilitative ideal" in favor of "retribution" as a purpose of prisons in the 1970s contributed to the explosion of incarceration during the 1980s. This helps to account for the increase in the number of female, poor, elderly, and terminally ill individuals now behind bars.

What societal purpose is served by punishing people who are sick or poor or old? As a nation, have we come to believe that such individuals deserve punishment more than support? If that is the case, it illustrates some troubling values held by our society.

Women Prisoners

The Bureau of Justice Statistics reported that of the 1.2 million Americans imprisoned in adult correctional facilities by the end of 1996, about 75,000 were women (Mumola & Beck, 1997). The same report indicated a disturbing increase in the number of females incarcerated. The study found that, in the preceding decade, "the annual rate of growth of female inmates has averaged 11.2%, higher than the 7.9% average increase in male inmates. By 1996 women accounted for 6.3% of all prisoners nationwide, up from 4.6% in 1985" (p. 5).

These women not only share a cell, they share a history. They are overwhelmingly poor, disproportionately minorities, less than 35 years old, and single. Over three fourths of them are mothers; two thirds have children under the age of 18. Nearly half of them reported communicating with their children from prison at least once a week.

More than 40% of the women reported having been physically or sexually abused, or both (Snell & Morton, 1994). Often the perpetrator of the abuse was an intimate partner or relative. Only three in ten women were incarcerated on violent charges, and often the victim had been an intimate partner or relative who had been abusive to the woman.

Many of the women in prisons are sick. Two thirds reported having used drugs regularly before their incarceration and over 40% used drugs daily. One in

mates, some requiring supplemental oxygen, dialysis, or tube feedings. Aside from continued punishment, it is difficult to ascertain what societal purpose is served by allowing terminally ill individuals to remain and die behind bars.

Conclusions

There is no question that prisons are harmful places (Clark, 1995; Halleck, 1971; Toch, 1992a, 1992b), even those that are managed well. They have become more harmful since abandoning any pretext of rehabilitation. For violent offenders, our society has not identified acceptable alternatives to prison, and most people believe that incapacitation is a legitimate reason to incarcerate those who hurt others. But why must we incarcerate individuals whose crimes are a result of their addictions or their poverty, or those who are elderly or dying? These are societal problems that are better addressed in alternative settings.

Prisons are not social welfare agencies. That is not their purpose. They are not funded to provide such services and are unlikely to produce beneficial results. For many mothers or poor or elderly or dying prisoners, there is no reason to keep them behind bars other than our seemingly increasing need for retribution. Imprisonment is costly, both in terms of the dollars spent and in terms of the shattered lives of the prisoners and the families they leave behind.

In the words of Thomas Jefferson—ironically quoted as a preface to *The National Drug Control Strategy, 1997* (Office of National Drug Control Policy, 1997)—"The care of human life and happiness, and not their destruction, is the first and only legitimate object of good government." Such words mandate that we seek other alternatives to imprisonment for what are, in essence, social problems.

References

Anno, B. J. (1991). *Prison health care: Guidelines for the management of an adequate delivery system.* Chicago: National Commission on Correctional Health Care.

Anno, B. J. (1997). Health behavior in prisons and correctional facilities. In D.S. Gochman (Ed.), *Handbook of health behavior research III* (pp. 289-303). New York: Plenum.

Bureau of Justice Statistics. (1996). *Sourcebook of criminal justice statistics-1995.* Washington, DC: Author.

Clark, J. (1995). The impact of the prison environment on mothers. *The Prison Journal, 75*(3), 306-329.

Halleck, S. L. (1971). Corrections in a democratic society. In J. Fawcett (Ed.), *Dynamics of violence* (pp. 43-57). Chicago: American Medical Association.

Hammett, T. M., Widom, R., Epstein, J., Gross, M., Sifre, S., & Enos, T. (1995). *1994 Update: HIV/AIDS and STDs in correctional facilities.* Washington, DC: National Institute of Justice.

Mumola, C. J., & Beck, A. J. (1997). *Prisoners in 1996.* Washington, DC: Bureau of Justice Statistics.

Office of National Drug Control Policy. (1997). *The national drug control strategy, 1997.* Washington, DC: Executive Office of the President.

Rafter, N. H. (1990). *Partial justice: Women, prison, and social control* (2nd ed.). New Brunswick, NJ: Transaction.

Simon, R. J., & Landis, J. (1991). *The crimes women commit, the punishment they receive.* Lexington, MA: Lexington Books.

Snell, T. L., &, Morton, D. C. (1994). *Women in prison* (Survey of state prison inmates, 1991). Washington, DC: Bureau of Justice Statistics.

Toch, H. (1992a). *Living in prison: The ecology of survival* (rev. ed.). Washington, DC: American Psychological Association.

Toch, H. (1992b). *Mosaic of despair: Human breakdowns in prison* (rev. ed.). Washington, DC: American Psychological Association.

von Hirsch, A. (1976). *Doing justice: The choice of punishments.* New York: Hill and Wang.

Weiner, J., & Anno, B. J. (1992). The crisis in correctional health care: The impact of the National Drug Control Strategy on correctional health services. *Annals of Internal Medicine, 117,* 71-77.

14

The "Epidemic" and "Cultural Legends" of Black Male Incarceration

The Socialization of African American Children to a Life of Incarceration

Tony L. Whitehead

Figure 14.1 Portrait of a prisoner.

Photograph by Lloyd DeGreen. Reprinted with permission.

U.S. Census Bureau demographers have projected that in 50 years, non-Hispanic whites will have dwindled to almost half (53%) of the total U.S. population. It is also estimated that Hispanics will have increased to about 25% of the U.S. population, and African Americans will rise to about 14%. In this chapter I argue that, given these demographic shifts, the United States, to remain a global leader, needs to seriously examine and address present conditions, policies, and practices in which prisons are emerging as a primary socializing institution of children within these nonwhite population groups. This chapter focuses on the problem as it particularly applies to African Americans. The data to support the points made in this chapter come from the existing literature and from comments of persons participating in a number of ethnographic studies that I directed over the past 10 years in inner-city communities in the Baltimore, Maryland/Washington, D.C. urban corridor (hereafter referred to as the "BW urban ethnographies"). The findings from our work should be considered suggestive and not confirmatory, due to varied and nonrandom methods of recruiting study participants, and varied methods of interviewing across studies. Nevertheless, the points made in this chapter are worthy of more systematic investigations to test how representative they might be in other low-income African American communities.

Over the past two decades, we have seen a rapid rise in U.S. incarceration rates, greatly accelerating during the past decade (Mauer, 1997a). What has been especially disturbing about the country's rush to incarcerate greater proportions of its population is that those being disproportionately incarcerated are African Americans—young black males in particular. Although African Americans make up only 12% of the total U.S. population, half of the U.S. prison population (51%) is black (Mauer, 1997b). African Americans are being imprisoned at seven times the rate of whites (Mauer & Huling, 1995). Studies have found across the United States that 33% of black men between the ages of 20 and 29 are either in prison or in jail, on probation, or on parole (Mauer & Huling, 1995). And in D.C. and Baltimore, 50% of young black men are under the jurisdiction of the judicial system.

Given the call from many sectors of American society for tougher crime laws and the construction of more jails and prisons, and the disproportionate incarceration of young black males, it is justifiable to examine this issue as an "epidemic," and to question how far society can go with the incarceration of young black men. Seventy-five percent? Ninety percent? Maybe even one hundred percent! Some might say that such projections are ludicrous. But they are in fact a reflection of how the present epidemic of black male incarceration fuels the long-held views of some in the African American community that U.S. policies, such as those contributing to this epidemic, are simply the latest strategy in an ongoing white-on-black genocidal plot, the master plan of whites to "solve the Negro problem." And whether one agrees or disagrees with this point of view, there is growing concern in the black communities in which I work about the impact this epidemic is having on their communities and families. At the same time, there is a growing awareness of the lack of proof that increased incarceration rates deter people, including previously incarcerated criminals, from committing more crimes (Mauer, 1997b, p. 2). There is also the awareness that such policies and practices do not necessarily prevent at-risk youth from becoming criminals in the first place (Raspberry, 1996). In fact, these communities are concerned about how these practices remove young men from their communities and send them back with felony records, enhanced aggressive and criminal behaviors, and AIDS.

Studies from many observers of the urban crime scene persistently find that increased incarceration does not deter drug trafficking, for which so many low-income African American and Hispanic youth are jailed, but merely inflames the anger and defiance of these young men. It has also been suggested that increased incarceration contributes to a "street culture" in which some young inner-city black males view the jail experience as a rite of passage into manhood (Anderson, 1994). Our findings from the BW urban ethnographies generally support these observations. Our work, however, suggests that there is a larger cultural context than that of a street culture, which we need to examine for a better understanding of the impact of the present day black male incarceration epidemic on young African American males, their families, and their communities. As the formation of culture is a process of historical reproduction, it is in the historical context of American race relations, and the shared stories or "cultural legends" that African Americans rely on for interpreting that history, that the impact of this epidemic on African Americans, and their reaction to it, can best be understood. Our research consistently suggests that to build more prisons, and jail more and more young people, in the absence of a more holistic or comprehensive approach to the problem of crime, which would consider these broader cultural contexts, may in fact be planting the seeds for increased crime and violence.

Although the incarceration of black males today has reached epidemic proportions, according to the comments of our study participants the phenomenon itself is not new. Indeed, some of their comments suggest that there exists among some African Americans a "cultural legend of black male incarceration." This legend holds that the jailing of black men by white men, although deeply resented, should be expected by black men as an historical "reality." As one study participant from our 1990-1991 urban drug trafficking study said to me, "You got the degrees. You know the history. Most of the laws of this country were created to control the black man. . . . If they can't find something to put your ass in jail for, and you continue being uppity, they kill your ass. That's what happened to Martin Luther King" (Whitehead, 1994).

The cultural legend of black male incarceration in the United States is similar to the "buccra-massa" (buck the master) complex, which I studied in the West Indies (Whitehead, 1984). Both of these legends emerged from the slave plantation histories of these societies, where the planter was the oppressor and the slave was the oppressed. The construct of the buccra-massa describes a discourse between the oppressor and the oppressed wherein slaves were physically tortured, caged, or killed because they had "bucked the master"; the master simply viewed the slaves as crazy for taking such risks. In current Jamaican social contexts, the buccra-massa complex has become a discourse between social classes, where "little people" (lower class) will not risk appearing defiant in the presence of a person of a higher class (Whitehead, 1984). In the U.S. context, the legend has remained one based primarily on race (rather than class) and gender: the white male is the persistent oppressor and the black male is the oppressed. Part of this black cultural legend holds that white men put black men in jail as an alternative to killing them. It also holds that those jailed are not necessarily incarcerated because they committed a crime. Instead, they may merely have acted defiantly or been tough. But because black men are so feared by white people, defiance and toughness are interpreted as threats to be put down. The legend has it that black men are caged because they have dared to—or it is feared that they will—buck the master. As one young study participant in our drug trafficking study commented, "The slave, sometime he didn't have to do nothing. He just had to look like he's bad, and his ass be dead" (Whitehead, 1994).

Part of this black cultural legend is that it is not only the lower income (little) black man who is subject to be jailed for bucking the master, but *no black man* can be allowed to get away with public displays of such defiance. Whereas upward mobility is a process into which Americans are socialized, those who are socialized into the legend of black male incarceration see a very fine balance between achieving higher status in American society and being seen as defiant or "uppity." This legend further holds that achieving higher socioeconomic status or power does not exempt the black man from being jailed, but could very well be interpreted as defiant or "bucking the master." As stated by one participant from the drug trafficking study, "See you got to remember, a nigger is just a nigger! That's what happened to Marion Barry [former D.C. mayor arrested in 1991 for crack cocaine possession and reelected in 1994]. He got too uppity—kept messing with them white boys. . . . I know they were going to one day catch him" (Whitehead, 1994).

Whereas acts that can be interpreted as bucking the master are seen as potentially bringing great risk, in the Jamaican setting little men (lower socioeconomic status) greatly admired other little men who took the risk (Whitehead, 1984). In the contemporary U.S. urban context, a similar admiration is held by some inner city youth. Spending time in jail has now become for some a symbol of black male strength and defiance. In two 1989-1990 AIDS-related studies, the concept of "Yo" or "Yo! Guy" was explained to me as a young male who wears expensive gold chains around his neck, designer brand-name (expensive) sweat suits and sneakers, and "stands around on the corner with his pants hanging down over his ass." The Yo's style of wearing expensive sweat suits that "hang down over his ass" is not only symbolic of his having the money to buy such clothes, but it is also symbolic of time spent in jail (pants hang low in jail because inmates' belts are taken away). It symbolizes that a young black man has "taken the white man's best shot" and is again on the streets, as defiant as ever (Whitehead, Peterson, & Kaljee, 1994). Understanding this symbolism provides a possible explanation of how, in a few months following his release from prison, Marion Barry quickly regained political power, first winning almost 90% of the vote for city councilman in a ward of predominantly lower income African Americans, then winning the 1994 mayoral election. He too had "taken the white man's best shot," and came out looking more fit, healthier, and more defiant than ever.

The benefits and risks of cultural legends are that they become part of the socializing process of the young. Cultural legends consist of beliefs and stories that are passed down from generation to generation, providing lessons of survival, strength, and the nature of the world around us. Children also enculturate these lessons by modeling others, both within and outside their communities, whom they see or hear acting out aspects of the legends. For example, models of crime, violence, and incarceration may not only be found among the Yo! Guys in their communities, but may be brought in through such popular media as television, movies, and rap music. The legends are strengthened for children by repeated events that demonstrate their veracity, such as the continuously increasing incarceration experiences of black males that they know or have heard about.

The black male incarceration epidemic has a socializing influence in other ways as well. Imprisonment can turn young people into more seasoned or hardened criminals. This theme was supported by one of our older street hustlers in the drug trafficking study, who explained that jail is an institution of continuing education for black men: ". . . It [jail] is like his training ground where he develops his skills for hustling when he be back on the street. . . . That's where he learns to become a criminal. . ." (Whitehead, 1994). The logic of this sentiment can be found in the fact that in several urban areas more young men are arrested than finish high school. For these young men, the prospects for formal education and opportunities for respectable and economically satisfying employment in the future are very limited. Jail is where many of the streetwise hustlers are concentrated. Moreover, it is a place in which a man can hone his skills without external distractions. Those reputational skills, such as being tough or running con games, will serve him well in the illegal hustles that might be his only economic opportunities when he returns to his inner-city community. Moreover, as explained by another older study participant, as difficult as jail can be, it can also be rewarding. For the poor black male, jail provides the opportunity to achieve reputational status among hardened male groups, and escape the responsibilities associated outside with respectable attributes that can never be achieved. As one study participant from a 1995 AIDS study commented, "You don't have to walk around with your head hanging down, not being able to face your women or your kids 'cause you can't get a job" (Whitehead, 1996).

The present black male incarceration epidemic is transforming the prospect of incarceration of black male children from simply that of a cultural legend to that of expected reality among some low-income residents of inner-city African American communities. An example of this transformation can be found in the statement made to me by one of our D.C. veteran street hustlers in the drug trafficking study: ". . . . [G]oing in and out of jail is part of the normal life cycle of any black man born and raised in D.C." This comment not only reflects the indigenous interpretation of the black male incarceration epidemic, it also reflects the concern of some of the community-based organizations with whom we work, who talk about the "revolving door" between black communities and prison, which further contributes to the spread of crime, violence, and AIDS as propagated in prison.

Another example of the present transformation of cultural legend to expected reality comes from the comments of young African American mothers in the drug trafficking study regarding attempts by the D.C. government to improve security in some public housing by installing fences between and around their developments. They were told that this was done to curtail the movement of those who commit acts of violence. But the young mothers with whom we talked, referring to the big strong iron fences, suggested that a continuous prison-like atmosphere had been created around their homes. As one young mother commented: "[O]ur children are being prepared for Lorton [the D.C. prison complex] even before they are old enough to commit a crime."

Yet another example of how the incarceration epidemic is becoming part of the conscious reality of young inner city residents came to light during a study of STD (sexually transmitted disease) risks among adolescent African American females (15 to 19 years old). These young women were asked, "What recommendations would you have for other young women your age, who have met a new boy with whom they are thinking of entering into a relationship?" Among the responses were: "make sure that the police isn't looking for him," or "make sure he didn't recently get out of jail" (Whitehead, 1997). Such comments suggest that the incarceration epidemic has now filtered into the decisions of young people regarding dating and mate selection, which in turn could affect their future marriages and formation of families. As such, this is a critical problem for the very survival of African Americans as a human community.

Anthropologists have long been interested in population survival in terms of intergenerational reproduction. One of the keys to the intergenerational survival of life forms that reproduce bisexually is sex ratios, or the proportion of males to females. There must be enough males and females within the population for a certain level of sexual bonding to occur and produce offspring who become fertile adults. The survival of human populations, however, requires more than biological fecundity. Human children must be nurtured in some type of family system so that they can become physically and mentally healthy adults. In the American ideal of the nuclear family, social parenting is as important to reproductive success as biological parenting. In other words, there are social parenting roles (mother and father) ascribed to the sexual partners giving birth to a child; how well those roles are played will have a significant effect on the physical and mental development of the child. The present incarceration epidemic of young black men, accompanied by the lack of employment and educational opportunities for this group, and death from the leading killers of this group—AIDS, homicide, and death by "legal intervention" (the U.S. Census Bureau's term for being killed in altercations with the police)—remove many of these young men from the potential pools of African American fathers, either biologically (through death) or socially. Having a prison record makes it difficult for young African American men to find stable work with a reasonable income or to secure a loan to buy a house. For such men, maximum economic capacity—an American ideal of masculinity—or even reasonable economic capacity often cannot be achieved through legal means. For some of these men, the hustling skills they learn in prison become useful and convenient for them in gaining respect as a man and being sexually and economically successful.

Yet such illegal activity raises their risk of being reincarcerated or killed, which in turn has a continuing negative impact on their ability to play the socially desired role of father. As such, the risk of lives of poverty, violence, and crime for the children that they have biologically fathered, as well as their children's children, increases. Their communities, too, are placed at greater risk for these social ills through the massive biological (by death) or social removal of these young men as functioning members of their communities. Their communities are also negatively affected by the contribution made by the incarceration epidemic to the broad socialization of the children within these communities into lives of crime, violence, more incarceration, or death. It is the intergenerational and broader impact of the black male incarceration epidemic on African American communities that brings me to conclude that, unless we find some way to bring an end to this epidemic, the periodic charges of white-on-black genocide may have some legitimacy.

References

Anderson, E. (1994, May). The code of the streets. *The Atlantic Monthly.*

Mauer, M. (1997a). *Americans behind bars: U.S. and international use of incarceration, 1995.* Washington, DC: The Sentencing Project.

Mauer, M. (1997b). *Intended and unintended consequences: State racial disparities in imprisonments.* Washington, DC: The Sentencing Project.

Mauer, M., & Huling, T. (1995). *Young black Americans and the criminal justice system: Five years later.* Washington, DC: The Sentencing Project.

Raspberry, W. (1996, January 22). Household hints for the prison problem. *The Washington Post,* p. A19.

Whitehead, T. L. (1984) The Buccra-massa personality and the little man broker in a Jamaican sugartown: Implications for community health and education programs. *Social Science & Medicine, 19*(5), 561-572.

Whitehead, T. L. (1994, December). *Cultural legends and the epidemic of black male incarceration: A public health problem in America.* Paper presented at the Conference on Housing Issues and Ethnography, sponsored by the U.S. Department of Housing and Urban Development, Howard University, Washington, DC.

Whitehead, T. L. (1996, March). *A focus group assessment of HIV/AIDS related communication issues among incarcerated populations in Maryland correctional facilities.* Report submitted to the Maryland State Department of Health and Mental Hygiene, Baltimore, MD.

Whitehead, T. L. (1997). Urban low income African American men, HIV/AIDS, and gender identity. *Medical Anthropologist Quarterly, 11*(4), 411-447.

Whitehead, T. L., Peterson, J., & Kaljee, L.(1994). The "hustle": Socioeconomic deprivation, urban drug trafficking, and low-income, African-American male gender identity. *Pediatrics, 93*(6), 1050-1054.

15

Adult Time for Adult Crime
A Sound Bite, Not a Sound Policy

Miriam A. Rollin

Children, including adolescents, are not just smaller versions of adults—they differ from adults in several psychosocial aspects that affect decision making (Cauffman & Steinberg, 1995, p. 1763). This research-supported and intuitively obvious fact is the premise on which numerous laws are based: laws that prohibit those under a certain age (usually age 16, 18, or 21) from driving a motor vehicle, buying tobacco products and alcoholic beverages, being employed, entering into enforceable contracts, serving in the armed forces, engaging in consensual sexual intercourse, voting in elections, and so forth. The fact that children are different from adults is also the premise on which the juvenile justice system is based: Children are less able to fully understand the consequences of their actions, less able to control their impulses, more vulnerable to harm at the hands of adults, and more able to be "turned around," given proper intervention to address whatever problems led to the undesirable behavior.

Although no efforts have been made to treat children more like adults in the numerous areas mentioned above (if anything, laws have moved in the opposite direction, e.g., increasing the minimum age for purchase of alcoholic beverages), there has been a major trend in the juvenile justice arena to try more children as adults, following the "adult time for adult crime" slogan and the newspaper headline-induced hysteria among the public and politicians. This is perhaps a surprising policy trend considering the current state of adult corrections in this country (i.e., why are we rushing to put more children into a system that is al-

most universally regarded as a failure with adult offenders?), but it is, nevertheless, the trend.

During the 1990s, the number of juvenile cases "waived" to adult criminal
court for trial and sentencing increased over 70% (DeFrances & Strom, 1997).
The number of children (under age 18) confined in adult prisons nearly doubled
(Parent, Dunworth, McDonald, & Rhodes, 1997). More than 40 states changed
their laws to try more children as adults (Sickmund, Snyder, & Poe-Yamgrata,
1997), and the U.S. Congress changed federal law in 1994 to try more children
as adults.[1] This trend in juvenile justice policy, although popular among politicians singing the "get tough" refrain on the campaign trail, has been shown by
research to be ineffective and even counterproductive. To understand how the
trial and incarceration of juveniles as adults is ineffective and counterproductive
justice policy, one should review both the goals of the criminal justice system
and the extent to which the policy of treating juvenile offenders like adults
achieves—or fails to achieve—those goals, and any other impacts of the policy.

Trying Children as Adults: Meeting
the Goals of the Justice System?

The goals of the criminal justice system are often described as falling into four
categories: punishment, incapacitation, deterrence, and rehabilitation. Trying
and incarcerating juveniles as adults is often viewed by politicians as a means of
punishing and incapacitating *violent* offenders. However, the majority of juveniles "waived" to adult criminal court have been—and remain—those alleged to
have committed either property or drug offenses, as opposed to violent offenses
(Butts, 1997). Trying juveniles as adults is also considered an effective strategy
for punishment and incapacitation by those who believe that juveniles tried as
adults are more likely to be incarcerated, and likely to be incarcerated for a
longer period. However, studies have found that juveniles were often handled no
more—and sometimes less—strictly by the adult criminal courts than by juvenile courts: Juveniles in criminal courts were less likely to be confined, and
when juveniles transferred to adult criminal courts were confined, they were not
generally confined for a longer period of time than similar offenders confined in
the juvenile justice system (Parent, Dunworth, McDonald, & Rhodes, 1997). Juveniles in adult courts are also less likely to be found guilty than their counterparts in juvenile court, and adult court processes are likely to take more time,
thereby delaying or preventing the "swift and sure" justice needed to more fully
realize the punishment and incapacitation goals (as well as the rehabilitation
goal) (Fagan, 1991).

Deterrence is an important justice system goal—one that is often mentioned
in the context of policies that try more juveniles as adults—but that goal is also
not served well by these policies. Research in two very different states (New

York and Idaho) has shown that "get tough" statutes to try more juveniles as adults (statutes providing for "legislative" or "automatic" waiver to adult court for certain offenses) have had no measurable deterrent effect on serious juvenile crime (Jensen & Metsger, 1994; Singer & McDowall, 1988). Another indicator of the failure of this policy to deter serious juvenile crime is that states with high rates of transferring children to adult court do not have lower rates of juvenile homicide (Lotke & Schiraldi, 1996).

The fourth justice system goal—rehabilitation—is not served by policies trying more children as adults; in fact, research has demonstrated that children tried as adults have a higher recidivism rate than closely matched children tried as juveniles. Children prosecuted as adults reoffend sooner, commit more serious new offenses, and reoffend more often than comparable children kept in the juvenile system (Bishop, Frazier, Lanza-Kaduce, & Winner, 1996; Fagan, 1991; Winner, Lanza-Kaduce, Bishop, & Frazier, 1997). This means that a policy of trying more children as adults not only fails to reduce crime but is actually likely to increase crime. This result is not surprising when one considers the realities for children living in adult jails, including the lack of needed educational, mental health, and social or family services (services which address the problems that led to the child's offenses in the first place) (Forst, Fagan, & Vivona, 1989), and the likely effect of children having incarcerated adult criminals as their pervasive adult role models (in their cells, during their meals and exercise periods, in the hallways, etc.).

Children in Adult Prisons: Risk of Harm

The risk of harm to children in the criminal justice system is widespread and troubling, considering that over two thirds of the states disperse children tried as adults and place them in adult prisons among the adult inmate population, as opposed to somehow segregating them from adult inmates in the prisons (Parent, Dunworth, McDonald, & Rhodes, 1997). Overall, children in adult jails are five times more likely to be sexually assaulted, twice as likely to be beaten by staff, and 50% more likely to be attacked with a weapon than children in a juvenile facility (Forst, Fagan, & Vivona, 1989). Furthermore, the suicide rate of juveniles in adult jails is 7.7 times higher than the rate among juveniles in detention centers (Flaherty, 1980).

Perhaps more compelling than the statistics are the real lives of children that have been shattered by experiences in adult jails. On April 25, 1996, 17-year-old Damico Watkins, who had been the lookout in a robbery attempt, was stabbed to death by six adult prisoners while incarcerated in an Ohio adult prison. On January 26, 1996, 16-year-old Rodney Hulin Jr., who had confessed to arson that caused $500 worth of damage to a fence, hanged himself in his Texas cell and went into a coma for four months before he died; prior to his suicide, he had been repeatedly beaten and sexually assaulted by adult prisoners. In Ohio, a 15-year-old girl, an A student who had never been in trouble before, ran away from home and returned voluntarily; she was put in jail by a judge to "teach her a lesson," where she was sexually assaulted by a guard on her fourth night in jail.[2]

Surely, these are not situations that this nation wants to repeat. And yet that is what this nation is likely to do, by trying more juveniles as adults and incarcerating more juveniles with adults.

Conclusion

Despite its popularity as a political mantra, "adult time for adult crime," trying and incarcerating more children as adults fails to realize any of the four justice system goals: punishment, incapacitation, deterrence, and rehabilitation. In fact, trying children as adults can actually backfire and lessen the likelihood of punishment, incapacitation, and rehabilitation. Furthermore, trying more children as adults has been shown to result in significant harm to those children, from physical and sexual victimization to murder and suicide.

We, as a nation, are at a turning point on this issue. We can stay on the ineffective and counterproductive path of trying and incarcerating more children as adults, or we can dare to reject the sound bites in favor of some sound policies: investments in prevention and alternatives to incarceration.

Notes

1. See the *Violent Crime Control and Law Enforcement Act of 1994*.
2. Cases from the files of the Youth Law Center, Washington, D.C., Mark Soler, President.

References

Bishop, D. M., Frazier, C. E., Conza-Kaduce, L., & Winner, L. (1996). The transfer of juveniles to criminal court: Does it make a difference?, *Crime & Delinquency, 42*, 171-191.

Butts, J. (1997). *Delinquency cases waived to criminal court, 1985-1994.* Fact Sheet #52. Washington, DC: Office of Juvenile Justice and Delinquency Prevention.

Cauffman, E. & Steinberg, L. (1995). The cognitive and affective influences on adolescent decision making. *Temple Law Review, 68*, p. 1763-1789.

DeFrances, C. J., & Strom, K. J. (1997). *Juveniles prosecuted in state criminal courts.* Washington, DC: Bureau of Justice Statistics.

Fagan, J. (1991). *The comparative impacts of juvenile and criminal court sanctions on adolescent felony offenders.* Washington, DC: National Institute of Justice.

Flaherty, M. G. (1980). *An assessment of the national incidence of juvenile suicide in adult jails, lock-ups and juvenile detention centers.* Urbana-Champaign: The University of Illinois at Urbana-Champaign, Community Research Forum.

Forst, M., Fagan, J., & Vivona, T. S. (1989). Youth in prisons and training schools: Perceptions and consequences of the treatment-custody dichotomy. *Juvenile and Family Court Journal, 40,* p. 1-14.

Jensen, E. L., & Metsger, L. K. (1994). A test of the deterrent effect of legislative waiver on violent juvenile crime. *Crime & Delinquency, 40,* p. 96-104

Lotke, E., & Schiraldi, V. (1996). *An analysis of juvenile homicides: Where they occur and the effectiveness of adult court intervention.* Alexandria, VA: National Center on Institutions and Alternatives and Center on Juvenile and Criminal Justice.

Parent, D., Dunworth, T., McDonald, D., & Rhodes, W. (1997). *Transferring serious juvenile offenders to adult courts.* Wasington, DC: National Institute of Justice.

Sickmund, M., Snyder, H. N., & Poe-Yamagata, E. (1997). *Juvenile offenders and victims: 1997 update on violence.* Washington, DC: Office of Juvenile Justice and Delinquency Prevention.

Singer, S., & McDowall, D. (1988). Criminalizing delinquency: The deterrent effects of the New York Juvenile Offender Law. *Law and Society Review, 22,* p. 521-535.

Winner, L., Lanza-Kanduce, L., Bishop, D. M., & Frazier, C. E. (1997). The transfer of juveniles to criminal court: Reexamining recidivism over the long term. *Crime & Delinquency, 43,* p. 548-563.

16

Mass Incarceration
A Public Health Failure

Robert L. Cohen

Prisons are built with stones of law, brothels with bricks of religion.
William Blake, "The Marriage of Heaven and Hell"

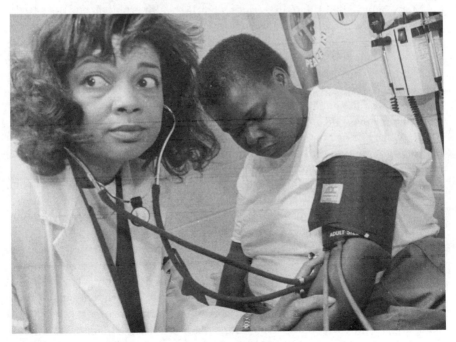

Figure 16.1 Doctor examines an inmate/patient.
Photograph by Meryl Levin. Reprinted with permission.

In 1991 the American Public Health Association (APHA) passed a resolution on the "Social Practice of Mass Imprisonment."[1] The APHA noted that prison health and community health were intimately related, that medical and mental health problems had a very high prevalence in prisons, and that imprisonment was racially and economically skewed. Noting that the "APHA has long defined drug abuse as a public health problem rather than a criminal justice problem," the resolution further asserted that the billions of dollars spent to imprison people would be used more effectively and efficiently by increasing drug treatment, halfway houses, and other alternatives to incarceration.

Many would agree with these statements. As their prisons have reached capacity, the policy of most states has been to increase the number of persons supervised in alternatives to incarceration. This does not, however, result in any decrease in the number of persons incarcerated. Rather, the total number of persons under state criminal surveillance (imprisonment, parole, probation, court-ordered drug treatment, boot camp) continues to rise at a frightening rate. There is no financial barrier to mass incarceration. No matter how expensive the policy of mass incarceration (alternative and traditional), it has never been found too expensive for any mayor, county executive, governor, or president.

Many believe that illicit drug use is a public health problem, and pose traditional public health solutions: drug treatment, social marketing, alternatives to incarceration, raising the standard of living, increasing employment, and decreasing hopelessness. Many public health workers have labored courageously and with little financial or emotional encouragement to help drug users end their dependence. But aspects of this approach to drugs have allowed social policy makers to use the public health model within the criminal justice system to legitimize the mass incarceration of drug users.

How can this be? Is there any support for the claim that there is an unspoken but malign intent to the public health perspective regarding drug use? Assume that there is no intent, but consider why drug users enter drug treatment.

Drug users have difficulty obtaining drugs because drugs are expensive and illegal. Sometimes the risk overwhelms the desire for drugs, or the drug user decides that drug use is personally destructive (this is often an age-related phenomenon) and stops using, with or without treatment.

Often, however, the work of obtaining illegal drugs results in infrequent but predictable encounters with armed men who are actually state agents posing as drug users. These encounters, facilitated by informers and characterized by entrapment, result in arrests followed by convictions. Some individuals are sentenced to drug treatment as an alternative. Although drug treatment programs do help some who wish to stop using drugs achieve their goal, many "fail" treatment, preferring the use of illegal drugs to abstinence. These predictable failures result in further encounters with the police, and, in some cases, court-mandated referrals to more highly supervised alternatives to incarceration, which are structured as drug treatment programs. Eventually, and with special attention to class status and skin color, incarceration is ordered as the treatment for the failure of drug treatment.

The complications of excessive drug use create a public health problem. Drug treatment is an alternative to incarceration. For those who fail treatment, the alternative is punishment to fit the crime. The support for mass imprisonment intrinsic in the usual public health approach to drugs may or may not be intentional, but it is substantial. The criminalization of drug use and the development of ever more draconian sentencing practices were the driving force for mass incarceration over the past 40 years. Why do we criminalize drug use? The drug most likely to cause violent behavior is alcohol, whereas opiates and marijuana are primarily sedating.

The United States criminalizes behavior differentially depending on the race and class of the potential criminal. Cocktail waiters were not incarcerated during alcohol prohibition. College students have rarely been imprisoned for smoking or selling marijuana. Young black men who use heroin and sell small quantities of drugs fill our jails and prisons. What distinguishes these groups from one another? Compare and contrast. Now.

Racial disparity in the administration of justice has always been a central feature of law enforcement in the United States. From slavery to lynching to the dramatic disparity in the use of the death penalty, poor black men have been continuously subjected to deadly inequity by the "justice system." In the case of the criminalization of drug use, the enormous racial disparities in arrest and conviction for these crimes is not accidental.[2]

Here's a little pop quiz:

Question:	When is it illegal to use drugs?
Answer:	When it is illegal.
Question:	Why is it illegal?
Answer:	Because it is against the law.

The joining of the moral and the medical which informs late 20th century ethical discussion is the ground that joins public health to the war on drugs. This connection, in which public health adopts as its own principle an arbitrary moral/legal principle—drug use is illegal, therefore drug use is against the public health—is substantially responsible for the public health support for mass incarceration as a legitimate treatment for the drug user who "fails" traditional drug treatment.

In the late 19th century, opium syrups were among the most popular home remedies. England fought a war to ensure that opium production, trade, and distribution were maintained. Marijuana was a staple crop with multiple industrial and medicinal uses, and alcohol, in its many forms, was freely available. The

United States, during the first quarter of the 20th century, led by religious groups that viewed the use of these substances as immoral, pursued a policy of drug use prohibition. These efforts were closely linked to nativist anti-immigrant and anti-Communist efforts in the immediate pre- and post-World War I era. The Volstead Act, which banned alcohol use, was passed during World War I.

The consequences of this policy have been profoundly destructive and deforming. Prohibition of alcohol quickly led to mass violence, dramatic development of organized criminal activity, mass police corruption, and generalized hypocrisy. The law was flaunted by every social class. Speakeasies operated freely, and huge fortunes flowed to the "legitimate" businessman who provided the alcohol to the "illegitimate" distributors. Prohibition of alcohol was abandoned as social policy after 13 years.

Yet prohibition of narcotics and marijuana is still the rule. Over the past 25 years, the number of people arrested for drug use has more than doubled, and the number of people imprisoned has more than tripled. These prisoners are overwhelmingly men of color, especially African Americans. The racism explicit in the policy of mass incarceration for illegal drug use cannot be ignored.

Prohibition is unwarranted and a failure. The public health consequences of the failure of prohibition are mass incarceration, epidemics of hepatitis B and hepatitis C, and rapid transmission of AIDS. Despite clear evidence that "needle exchange" prevents the transmission of AIDS among injecting drug users, the federal government refuses to support this policy. Why?

Public health demonizes drug use as drug abuse. To support a needle exchange policy, the public health community had to demonstrate first that needle exchange decreased the incidence of AIDS, and second, that needle exchange did not increase the incidence of drug use. Most studies supported the first premise. Proving the second was much more difficult. The denial of federal support for needle exchange was based on a calculus in which the "danger" of potential drug use outweighed the public benefit of preventing AIDS. This is essentially a public health argument, encompassing epidemiological evidence and risk-benefit analysis, even though the conclusion is contrary to general public health support for needle exchange.

The right approach to drugs is to tolerate them when they are safe, and to minimize harm for higher risk drug use. The United States has the highest incarceration rate in the world, specifically because of its policy on drugs. This policy currently allocates 16 billion federal dollars to the war on drugs, and mandates tougher sentences and "supermax" prisons. Western Europe provides many successful models of drug policies that seek to reduce harm, and result in lower rates of violence, property crime, and serious complications of drug use.[3] A national policy of harm reduction, coupled with an appropriate public health model which teaches harm reduction rather than punitive treatment, will save both lives and enormous sums of money.

Ask yourself the following questions: Is half a million prisoners enough? Is one million prisoners enough? Is one in three black men under the age of 30 under state criminal custody or alternative sentencing enough? Today there are nearly 2 million persons in jails and prisons in the United States, four times the number 20 years ago. The largest majority are black men locked up because they use drugs. When is enough enough?

William Blake's insight of 200 years ago resonates today. Blake understood how moral and religious principles are the foundation for the social construction of criminal behavior. When the law, religion, and public health get together, better watch out.[4] Collusively, coercively, and mistakenly, they identify drug use as criminal, and provide the justification for punishment.

Anybody want a drink?

Notes

1. Resolution #9123, available from APHA, 800 I Street, NW, Washington, DC 20001-3710; phone (202) 777-2742.

2. Randall Kennedy in his book *Race, crime, and the law,* Pantheon, 1997, demonstrates calmly and chillingly the manner in which "justice" has been unfairly administered in the United States based on race.

3. Nadleman, Ethan. (1998, January-February). Commonsense drug policy. *Foreign Affairs, 77,* No. 1.

4. See also Richards, D. A. (1982). *Sex, drugs, death and the law: An essay on human rights and overcriminalization.* Totowa, NJ: Rowman and Littlefield.

17

Detention of Migrants

Fernando Chang-Muy

Some of the most vulnerable people in U.S. prisons are those who have migrated from abroad. Some have left their countries for economic reasons, others have fled because of political upheavals. The "poor, tired" and those "yearning to be free"[1] are now photographed, fingerprinted, detained, or expeditiously removed if they enter without proper documents. Once incarcerated, the migrant population often faces more trouble and difficulties than do violent criminals.

Migrants and Refugees

The United States grew and developed in part by migration. The early settlers from England came for economic reasons, as did many of their later successors from Europe—most notably from Ireland, Italy, and Poland. The pilgrims who landed at Plymouth Rock, however, were not detained, unlike many who now arrive. Today's migrants come for many of the same economic reasons that drove the colonists out of England, but these latter-day migrants hail from different continents and different areas—Asia, Africa, Russia, Latin America. Now, temporary or permanent migration status is achieved only through strict, limited, and narrow channels, typically restricted to family and labor sponsorship conditions.

Refugees are also migrants. They don't leave their homelands for economic reasons, but out of fear of persecution on account of race, religion, nationality, social group, or political opinion. The office of the United Nations High Commissioner for Refugees estimates that there are more than 14 million refugees around the world ("State of the World's Refugees," 1998). One in every 122 people on earth has been forced into flight. They often leave without documents because they do not have time to secure them or they are afraid of their government and reluctant to go to their Ministry of State for passports. Thus, some refugees flee and try to enter the United States with false documents.

Incarceration

Migrants are permitted legal entry into the United States only with proper documents. When refugees are discovered at the border (e.g., in airports) without proper documents, however, the United States either immediately deports or detains them.[2] If, after an immigration hearing (often held within the walls of the prison), the immigration judge deems that the person is indeed a refugee, the person is released and can become a lawful permanent resident after one year.

Deterrence of illegal immigration is one of the main policy objectives governing the detention of migrants. Congress has recently enacted and amended many laws to strengthen the response to persons in violation of its immigration laws. The Department of Justice's Immigration and Naturalization Service (INS) implements these legislative mandates. The laws result in the detention of people seeking refuge (asylum seekers), undocumented migrants, and long-term permanent residents with a criminal record. While awaiting deportation proceedings, any noncitizen convicted of virtually any criminal offense, even a minor one (including those individuals who entered the country legally) is to be detained without bond, as mandated by these same laws. In some cases, the sentence for the criminal conviction is completed long before the deportation hearing.

Facilities

In 1997, on average the INS had 13,600 persons in detention on any given day. At that time, the agency directly managed nine detention facilities. In addition, six facilities were operated by private for-profit companies, and two facilities for criminal migrants were operated jointly by the INS and the Federal Bureau of Prisons. The majority of immigration detainees, however, are imprisoned under contract with the federal government in over 500 state and county jails. This has cost the Justice Department over $1.1 billion during the past three years ("Detention Resource Manual," 1998).

Issues Surrounding Detention

The problems faced by all inmates of U.S. jails and prisons are frequently compounded for migrants. For most, their only offense was entering the country without proper documents. Most do not have a criminal background. Yet adults and juveniles, men and women, find themselves housed with persons convicted of all types of crimes, including violent acts. Despite their situation, the migrants have no right to a government-appointed lawyer because immigration issues are considered civil law.

The setting for these state and county prisons is typically far removed from the urban settings where the migrants' supporters, families, and legal representation reside. This leads to social isolation and disrupts any social support networks. Furthermore, because of the remote location of these prisons, the prison guards and staff are usually culturally homogeneous, and often unfamiliar with the migrants' culture. Communication barriers caused by language differences can create many problems and even lead to danger for the detainees and staff. Although the INS has developed some standards and protocols governing the conditions of immigration detainees, these standards apply only to the INS-operated facilities, not the contracted state and county facilities.

Perhaps because of the vulnerable legal status of immigration detainees, violence perpetuated against them is particularly problematic. For example, in a 1998 decision, a jury convicted one prison guard and acquitted another in the abuse of immigrants at the Union County Jail in New Jersey. It was the reported testimony of approximately two dozen immigrants in two trials that Union County Jail guards chanted, "America is number one," while punching and kicking them. One immigrant said a guard grabbed his penis with a set of pliers, and several said their heads were pushed into toilets and they were forced to kneel naked against other detainees (Detention Watch Network News, 1998).

Consequences

Immigration detainees endure and experience conditions designed for those who have victimized individuals or society, and often more. Only recently has the incorporation of migrants into our society been viewed as a victimization of our society. Although many communities have not been historically kind to migrants, the government protected them, and others came to appreciate and benefit from their talents and hard work.

Today, the policy in the United States of detaining migrants, coupled with the various driving forces of economics and politics, has resulted in a prison population in which, by and large, First World keepers and guards imprison Third World people. The disruption of social connections and the infliction of violent conditions has a lasting impact on those who journey through the detention system and are ultimately released. This impact is felt by tens of thousands of individuals and families each year in the United States and abroad, and has the potential to build dissent. "The United States is acting as if they didn't know the world was round," stated one African (personal communication).

The Statue of Liberty should continue to welcome those in need, not symbolize the detention of those yearning to be free between her shores.

Notes

1. From Emma Lazarus' poem, which is on the pedestal of the Statue of Liberty.
2. According to the 1996 Anti-Terrorism and Effective Death Penalty Act (AEDEPA) and the 1996 Illegal Immigration Reform and Immigrant Responsibility Act (IRRAIRA) passed by Congress, asylum seekers without documents must express a credible fear of persecution upon their arrival in the United States. Those who do not are expeditiously removed and deported. Those who do express such a fear are detained, and must wait in prison until an asylum hearing is conducted and the case is decided.

References

Lutheran Immigration and Refugee Service. (1998). *Detention resource manual.* New York: Author.

Lutheran Immigration and Refugee Service. (1998, February). *Detention Watch Network News,* Issue 4. New York: Author.

Office of the United Nations High Commissioner for Refugees. (1998). *The state of the world's refugees—A humanitarian agenda.* Geneva, Switzerland: Author.

Suggested Readings

International:

United Nations High Commissioner for Refugees. *Guidelines on Detention of Asylum Seekers.* UNHCR IOM12/96 FOM No. 11/96. Geneva, Switzerland: Author.

United States:
8 US Code

1996 Anti-Terrorism and Effective Death Penalty Act (AEDEPA) (P.L No. 104-132).
1996 Illegal Immigration Reform and Immigrant Responsibility Act (IRRAIRA) (P.L. No. 104-208).

8 Code of Federal Regulations
INS Memos and cases:

Detention use policy, July 14, 1997.
Unaccompanied minors and expedited removal, August 21, 1997.
Cubans in indefinite detention cases.
Flores v. Meese, unaccompanied minors.

Journal articles and publications:

Lutheran Immigration and Refugee Service. *Detention resource manual.* (1998). New York: Author.

Lutheran Immigration and Refugee Service. *Detention Watch Network News.* (1998). New York: Author.

Taylor, M. (1997). Promoting legal representation for detained aliens: Litigation and administrative reform. *Connecticut Law Review, 29,* 1647.

Taylor, M. (1995). Detained aliens challenging conditions of confinement and the porous border of the Plenary Power Doctrine. *Hastings Constitutional Law Quarterly, 32,* 1087.

18

Mental Illness Behind Bars

Andrea Weisman

In the United States today more than twice as many people who are seriously mentally ill receive services in jails and prisons than in public psychiatric hospitals. An estimated 1.7 million people are in jails and prisons and, even if 8% of those are seriously mentally ill, a conservative but frequently cited estimate, this translates to a mentally ill population of approximately 135,000 (Bureau of Justice Statistics, 1998). In comparison, in 1994 there were only about 70,000 patients in the nation's public psychiatric hospitals, and today there are even fewer (Torrey, 1997). Some researchers hold the figure in jails to be closer to 9% for men and 18.5% for women (Butterfield, 1998; Teplin, 1994). Even these percentages are probably underestimates, because the methodologies for such studies and jail screening processes generally overlook individuals who have not previously received mental health services or who present themselves as quiet and withdrawn even though they are quite ill (Teplin, 1997).

Many of the most seriously mentally ill have been dropped from the rolls of the public mental health system as it has shrunk services and lessened accessibility through such policy shifts as deinstitutionalization, stringent involuntary commitment criteria, and managed behavioral health care initiatives. Significant numbers wind up homeless and at increased risk for arrest (Torrey et al., 1992). It is estimated that the number of seriously mentally ill people who are incarcerated may be as high as 40% of all seriously mentally ill people in the United States (Torrey, 1997). Supporting this estimate is a study in which approximately 1,400 randomly selected members of National Alliance for the Mentally Ill (NAMI) were interviewed; 40% reported having been arrested at some point in their lives (Steinwachs, Kaspar, & Skinner, 1992). Among the mentally ill who are homeless, the arrest rate is even higher. In a study of 200 homeless people in Los Angeles, as many as 74% reported a previous arrest (Gelberg, Linn, & Leake, 1988).

Jails and prisons have become the de facto providers of mental health services in this country. In fact, the largest provider of mental health services in the United States, in terms of annual patient contacts, is the Los Angeles County Jail. The largest provider of mental health services in most states is the state prison system. The problem, of course, is that jails and prisons are not, either by intent or design, therapeutic environments. The director of mental health services at the Los Angeles county jail says, "The whole concept of treatment in jail is an oxymoron. [Jail] is a horrible place... not good for people who are well. For someone who is mentally ill it is terrible" (Butterfield, 1998, p. A1). As Torrey expressed it, "Being in jail or prison when your brain is working normally is, at best, an unpleasant experience. Being in jail or prison when your brain is playing tricks on you is often brutal" (Torrey, 1997, p. 31).

The psychological consequences of being a homeless, seriously mentally ill person are devastating: hearing voices, feeling intensely paranoid, having difficulty thinking clearly, neither eating nor sleeping properly (or at all), and the risk of arrest for actions as simple as urinating outdoors. Once in jail, a mentally ill person is usually processed and housed alongside all others, including those who are stronger, perhaps even predatory, and those charged with violent felonies. In some facilities, mentally ill inmates are placed in brightly colored jumpsuits to designate their special status, yet this makes them more visible, vulnerable targets. Correctional officers who are poorly equipped to differentiate between obstinate refusals and floridly psychotic behavior often escalate confrontations with disruptive individuals by using unnecessary verbal or physical force to gain compliance. In addition, other inmates who become annoyed or irritated with the irregular behavior of a mentally ill fellow inmate might react aggressively. As a consequence, the mentally ill are more likely to be physically harmed and to be placed in administrative segregation or solitary confinement.

Security and custody decisions often thwart the provision of treatment to the mentally ill in correctional facilities. For example, inmates on "special handling" status are prohibited from participating in group therapy, a security directive that nevertheless undermines treatment possibilities. Similarly, court releases and sentencing—without adequate development of post-release treatment plans—can be a major obstacle to providing effective services for the mentally ill, even though they appear to be in the individual's immediate self-interest. Disrupted services are routine even among those requiring continuing care: Newly admitted detainees started on psychotropic medications or placed on suicide watch can easily slip through system cracks when released by the court without referrals to community-based agencies or service providers. Outcomes can be disastrous. If they are not taking their psychiatric medications, the seriously mentally ill are at an increased risk for violence, particularly if they use drugs or alcohol ("Note About Violence," 1998). As complicated as these case management concerns are, the characteristics of the culture of corrections present even more problems for mental health professionals. From the sights, sounds, and smells that assault the senses in correctional facilities, to the dehumanizing consequences of even usual conditions of confinement (such as living in cages, tasteless food or worse, enforced idleness, organized chaos, and violence among inmates and between staff and inmates), correctional environments are emotionally virulent settings. The psychological consequences of these environments are harmful to all those who live or work within them, not just those who are already mentally ill when they enter. Indeed, even people who are not mentally ill can become so after protracted stays in these environments.

Demonstration of the pathogenic consequences of correctional environments has principally focused on the most extreme conditions of confinement, because they are more discreet and therefore easier to delineate and investigate. Prolonged periods of solitary confinement in management control units or "supermax" facilities can have disastrous consequences for personality structure and organization. Hallucinations, irrational anger, confusion of thought, violent fantasies, hypersensitivity to stimuli, or, in contrast, emotional flatness, social withdrawal, and chronic depression are among the symptoms regularly seen in individuals confined under these extraordinary circumstances (see, e.g., Grassian, 1983; Grassian & Friedman, 1986). Although researchers are beginning to focus on the immediate consequences for confined individuals, few keep data on the total number of supermax isolation cells constructed, the number of individuals held in them, the duration of their confinement, or the longer-term consequences for both the inmates and officers who spend weeks, months, and years within these settings.

Studies of the pathogenic consequences of the *standard* conditions of confinement are even more challenging. That the "culture of oppression" has become ubiquitous makes measurement problematic. "(T)he variability and subjectivity of psychological pain has impeded the development of a standardized metric with which to gauge it. . . . Attempts to document the harmful effects of long-term imprisonment also are complicated by the fact that people may adapt over time to the suffering they endure" (Haney, 1997, p. 531).

In a study conducted more than 20 years ago, Zimbardo and colleagues at Stanford University demonstrated the malignant consequences of assuming the correctional roles of inmate, officer, and administrator (Haney & Zimbardo, 1977; Zimbardo & Musen, 1992). Though the study was to have been conducted over several weeks, it was forced to an abrupt end as the students and professors enacting their parts completely lost perspective on the fabricated nature of the enterprise: Within a week's time some became sadistic, cruel, and abusive, others became constricted and withdrawn, and still others suffered "nervous break-downs." Even this limited and contrived "prison" study was sufficient to induce participants to lose themselves in the scenario of absolute power and control, colored by mistrust and deception. In academic quarters, the extreme conse-quences for participants in this experiment brought to a head ethical concerns re-garding informed consent of subjects, and led to the development of human sub-jects review committees on university campuses.

Real inmates live in perpetual fear of being raped or beaten by officers or other inmates, of having their cells "popped" by officers so other inmates can as-sault them, and of being forced to participate in gladiator-like contests ("blood sport") and fights to entertain officers (Arax & Gladstone, 1998). Female in-mates may be forced to perform sexual acts on officers or on other inmates for officers' viewing pleasure (*Women Prisoners v. District of Columbia,* 1994). For officers, there may be equally pathogenic consequences from working in an en-vironment in which inmates throw feces or urine on them, and regularly engage in self-mutilation.

Toxic environments engender malignant outcomes. The amount of violence in correctional settings is more than five times that of the "free world." In 1995, the Bureau of Justice Statistics recorded a total of 40,000 assaults on staff or in-mates in correctional facilities, or 4% of the one million people incarcerated at that time (U.S. Department of Justice, 1997). In 1994, the rate of violent assaults in the general population was 0.7% of the population (Federal Bureau of Investi-gation, 1998).

Additionally, there is a dramatic increase in self-directed violence in correc-tional settings. Jails and prisons are the only environments in which swallowing a razor blade or hanging oneself may be "adaptive." Whereas these behaviors would be interpreted as indicators of serious psychopathology in the "free world," in correctional settings self-injurious behaviors are frequently staged to effect legal outcomes, obtain housing assignments, receive out-of-cell time, transfer to a more commodious psychiatric hospital, and get permission to make phone calls, among other desired outcomes. In correctional settings, these be-haviors are adaptive because they have an acquired currency; they have become correctional chits.

One third of all individuals in jails and prisons today—more than half a mil-lion people—are parole or conditional release violators (Bureau of Justice Sta-tistics, 1998). Perhaps the only sure result of being incarcerated is being reincar-cerated. If we want our criminal justice policy to perpetuate violent behavior and illness for reasons such as ensuring the continued profitability of correctional industry benefactors and corporate stakeholders, we should do nothing to change the status quo, because our policies and correctional environments guar-antee their own survivability in perpetuity. If, however, our aim is to build a sys-tem that contributes to improved outcomes for individuals and their communi-

Part IV

The Crucible of Violence

Prisons can be violent and toxic environments. Few come out of the prison experience unchanged, and most face enormous obstacles to successful assimilation into society. The following chapters describe the violence and abuses that mar prisons and prisoners, violence that is then carried into the community.

19

Sanctioned Violence in American Prisons

Steve J. Martin

Figure 19.1   Armed correctional officer patrolling the cellhouses in a Illinois prison.
Photograph by Lloyd DeGreen. Reprinted with permission.

*[P]leasure in cruelty is really not extinct today; only, given our greater deli-
cacy, that pleasure has had to undergo a certain sublimation. It has to be
translated into imaginative and psychological terms in order to pass muster
before even the tenderest hypocritical conscience.*
                                    —Nietzsche, *The Genealogy of Morals*[1]

The use of physical force to control prisoners is commonly employed in the
day-to-day administration of American prisons and jails. For example, in 1992,
the Texas prison system recorded over 6,300 major applications of force, or one
for every nine inmates (Texas Department of Criminal Justice, 1993). In 1996, in
the Central Punitive Segregation Unit of the New York City Department of Corrections, there were over 250 major applications of force, including 100 head injuries, for a population of 400 prisoners (*Sheppard v. Phoenix,* 1997). Such major applications of force are inherently dangerous to both prisoners and staff,
especially when weaponry such as batons, chemical agents, and projectiles are
employed. Consequently, this area of correctional administration is frequently
subject to court scrutiny, not only because of the potential for serious injury, but
also because the legitimate need to use force is often subject to abuse.

When force is applied for the very purpose of inflicting punishment and pain,
such an application constitutes de facto corporal punishment, but the use of corporal punishment in American corrections was effectively banned in 1968 as a
result of *Jackson v. Bishop* (1968). The plaintiffs in *Jackson* were prisoners in
the Arkansas prison system who had been subjected to whippings with a leather
strap that was some three feet long, four inches wide, and one quarter inch thick.
Then Circuit Judge Blackmun (later elevated to the Supreme Court) concluded
that "the strap's use, irrespective of any precautionary conditions which may be
imposed, offends contemporary concepts of decency and human dignity and
precepts of civilization which we profess to possess; and that it violates those
standards of good conscience and fundamental fairness enunciated by this
Court. . ." (*Jackson v. Bishop,* 1968, p. 579). The American Correctional Association also prohibits corporal punishment, but authorizes the use of force only
when no reasonable alternative is possible and then only the minimal force necessary (American Correctional Association, 1985). It is not uncommon, however, for ostensibly lawful applications of physical force to mask the intentional
infliction of punishment on prisoners by correctional personnel. Manufacturing
or exaggerating the need to physically control a prisoner is one means by which
staff use force as a pretext for inflicting punishment on a prisoner, thereby cir-
cumventing the constitutional prohibition on such physical punishments.

Many contemporary prison systems routinely employ a wide range of high
tech nonlethal weaponry during applications of force. Ironically, such weap-

onry, purportedly employed to minimize injuries to both staff and inmate, includes some that does not usually result in detectable injuries, even when misused by personnel, such as electronic immobilizing equipment (e.g., stun guns). This weaponry, however, almost always causes some degree of pain to the prisoner on whom it is employed.

The popularity of such weaponry in American corrections has risen just as the use of "supermax" prisons to house "super-predators" have come into vogue. This high tech weaponry is most often used on these demonized super-predators. Contemporary corrections officials have at their disposal such high tech nonlethal weaponry as electronic stunning devices, some of which are capable of delivering 50,000 volts and can be used with shields, darts, or probes, not unlike the "Tucker Telephone," which was a hand-cranked device used in the Arkansas prison system as late as the 1960s to deliver electric shocks to sensitive body parts such as the genitalia. Corrections officials also have sting shot rubber bullets, stun guns (canvas bags filled with lead shot; tear gas canisters filled with wood blocks or rubber pellets), "pepper spray" (a type of tear gas made from cayenne peppers developed in Canada to control bears), and a variety of restraint devices such as the restraint chair and the "Body Guard" (advertised as a "revolutionary new design that allows officers to safely restrain and immobilize combative subjects without facing the complications and dangers associated with the traditional restraint methods like hog-tying"[2]).

Regarding weaponry that leaves no obvious physical injuries, U.S. Supreme Court Justice Blackmun in his concurring opinion in *Hudson v. McMillian* (1992) concluded as follows:

> The Court today appropriately puts to rest a seriously misguided view that pain inflicted by an excessive use of force is actionable under the 8th Amendment only when coupled with "significant injury," e.g., injury that requires medical attention or leaves permanent marks. Indeed, were we to hold to the contrary, we might place various kinds of state-sponsored torture and abuse—of the kind ingeniously designed to cause pain but without a telltale "significant injury"—entirely beyond the pale of the Constitution. In other words, the constitutional prohibition of "cruel and unusual punishments" then might not constrain prison officials from lashing prisoners with leather straps, whipping them with rubber hoses, beating them with naked fists, shocking them with electric currents, asphyxiating them short of death, intentionally exposing them to undue heat or cold, or forcibly injecting them with psychosis-inducing drugs. Those techniques, commonly thought to be practiced outside this Nation's borders, are hardly unknown within this Nation's prisons. (p. 1002)

That these practices cited by Justice Blackmun in 1992 are a but a relic of times past is belied by a federal district court decision rendered in 1995 involving one of the nation's most modern high-tech supermax facilities operated by the California Department of Corrections, the Pelican Bay State Prison. This facility was touted as the prison of the future, employing cutting-edge technology with state-of-the-art security devices. The Pelican Bay State Prison security force had at their disposal a wide of array of nonlethal weaponry such as tasers (both handheld and projectile darts), handheld aerosols dispensing Mace, and tear gas canisters filled with wood block and rubber pellet projectiles fired at high velocity from a 37mm gas gun. But among the conditions of confinement challenged by the prisoners at Pelican Bay State Prison in a class action lawsuit was that staff routinely engaged in the unnecessary and wanton infliction of pain and the use of excessive force (*Madrid v. Gomez,* 1995).

The *Madrid* court found "that the extent to which force is misused at Pelican Bay, combined with the flagrant and pervasive failures in defendants' systems for controlling the use of force reveal more than just deliberate indifference: they reveal an affirmative management strategy to permit the use of force for the *purposes of punishment and deterrence*" [italics added] (*Madrid v. Gomez,* 1995, p. 1199). Excessive and unnecessary force at Pelican Bay was used in a variety of circumstances and settings. Prisoners were left naked in outdoor holding cages during inclement weather. Fetal restraints and "hog-tying" were commonplace. Beatings occurred even after restraint, and verbal harassment and racial taunting ensued. Prisoners were shot for fistfights both on the outdoor recreation yards and inside the cell blocks. One mentally ill prisoner suffered second and third degree burns over one third of his body when he was given a bath in scalding water in the prison infirmary one week after he had bitten an officer. Injuries sustained by prisoners ranged from lost teeth and fractures to fatal gunshot wounds.

Many of these practices are clearly employed sadistically and maliciously to inflict punishment on prisoners. One of the most insidious patterns of unnecessary and excessive force at Pelican Bay involved cell extractions carried out and sanctioned under the pretext of addressing legitimate security goals, such as recovering contraband. In one example, a prisoner had refused to relinquish his dinner tray. He was unarmed, locked securely in his cell, and weighed some 130 pounds. A cell extraction team of five officers and a sergeant, prior to entering the cell, discharged two multiple baton rounds hitting the prisoner in the groin, dispensed two bursts of Mace, and then fired two taser cartridges. The team then entered the cell and "restrained [the prisoner] after a brief struggle." (*Madrid v. Gomez,* 1995, p. 1280). In 1996, inside the New York City Central Punitive Segregation Unit, 40 inmates sustained head injuries in 50 incidents in which inmates were handcuffed, usually behind the back. This number of head injuries on restrained inmates is quite staggering, considering that properly trained correctional staff should be able to control a cuffed inmate without inflicting head injuries. Another particularly extreme and unusual feature of the use of force in the New York facility was the prevalence of perforated eardrums. From July

1989 through 1995, 33 inmates sustained confirmed or possible perforated or ruptured eardrums during use of force by correctional officers (*Sheppard v. Phoenix,* 1997).

As we are now fully ensconced in the age of the "supermax prison" in which we house "super-predators" in a "no frills" environment after they have had "three strikes," use of force is more easily sanctioned and justified than it otherwise would be. However, the basic rule of law that governs the use of excessive or unnecessary force in prisons and jails is no less applicable to the "worst of the worst" than to any other confined person. Moreover, although the courts should remain reluctant to superintend the day-to-day operation of corrections facilities, they must also remain reluctant to embrace the tautology that allows corrections professionals to modify the rule of law that governs the use of force in such a way that it can be used to *punish* prisoners rather than *control* them. As so eloquently suggested by the prisoners' attorney in her opening statement in *Madrid,* "[W]e, the people, are [not] free to act lawlessly because the people that we brutalize themselves have violated the law."[3]

Notes

1. Nietzsche, F. (1956/1887). *The genealogy of morals.* Garden City, NY: Doubleday Anchor Books, p. 200.
2. Advertisement for The Body Guard™ Restraining Systems.
3. Susan Creighton, in her Opening Statement, p. 1-28 of trial transcript.

References

American Correctional Association. (1985, January). *Public correctional policy on use of force.* Lanham, MD: Author.

Hudson v. McMillian, 112 S.Ct. 995, 1002 (1992).

Jackson v. Bishop, 404 F. 2d 571 (8th Cir. 1968).

Madrid v. Gomez, 889 F. Supp. 1146 (N.D. Cal. 1995).

Sheppard v. Phoenix, 91 CIV. 4148 (RPP). United States District Court, Southern District of New York, December 1, 1997.

Texas Department of Criminal Justice. (1993). *Report to the Texas Department of Criminal Justice—Internal Affairs and the Use of Force in Texas Department of Criminal Justice, Institutional Division.* Huntsville, TX: Author.

20

Even Dogs Confined to Cages for Long Periods of Time Go Berserk

Corey Weinstein

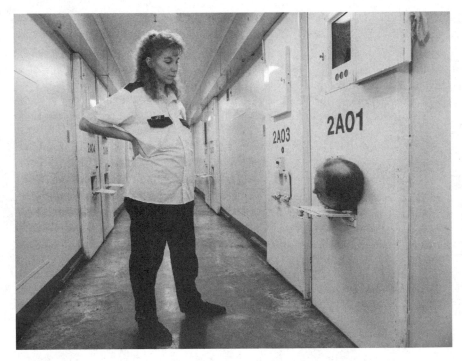

Figure 20.1 An inmate tries to communicate through the feeding slot of his isolation unit.

Photograph by Lloyd DeGreen. Reprinted with permission.

A first-time prisoner is horrified that a clique of guards is using the elected leader of the prisoner advisory council to run drugs into the various housing units of a maximum security prison. The prisoner gets himself elected to the advisory council and puts a stop to the drug running. The guards proceed to set him up for a fight, beat him and shoot pepper spray up his nose, and then get disciplinary charges against him that result in his removal to the Security Housing Unit for a two-year term in that isolation unit.

As told to the author by the affected prisoner,
California State Prison at Corcoran

When administrators within most Departments of Corrections (DOC) are asked why they need to build large, freestanding, 23-hour-a-day lock-up units, they respond that these "control units" are needed to house the "worst of the worst" prisoners in one place. By isolating those who assault staff or other inmates, or who habitually break rules, the rest of the prison system *is* temporarily safer. There is a reasonable logic to the assertion that, in our overcrowded prisons, filled with idle and often hopeless and desperate men and women, some must be isolated for the good of the many. But one outside investigation after another betrays this party line, and reveals the actual dark intent of control units. These units, like all aspects of prison life, serve an inner reasoning of the insular and defiant institution we call, erroneously, corrections.

Along with the explosion of prison building in the last 20 years has come the construction of control unit prisons in 41 states, the District of Columbia, and the Federal Bureau of Prisons.[1] State-of-the-art equipment is used for video and audio surveillance in these fully automated facilities. All movement is monitored and assisted by electronic door systems. Special alarms and security devices abound. Conditions in these segregation units include 23-hour-a-day lockup; solitary confinement (or double celling, rarely small group confinement); limited or no access to educational, vocational, or religious programs; and no employment opportunities. There are no congregate activities of any kind. Meals are eaten in the cell. No pictures can be put up on the cell walls, and personal property and reading materials are severely restricted. Guards perform all the service work, as no other prisoners are allowed in the units. Visits with family and friends are noncontact behind glass partitions, and usually limited to one or two hours at a time, a few days a week. Prisoners are strip-searched whenever they are moved from the unit, handcuffed before exiting their cells, and placed in full shackles with waist and hobble chains any time they are removed from the unit. There is no human contact, and solid door fronts, other design features, and special rules limit conversations among prisoners. This reduced environmental stimulation and social isolation is punishment for various rule violations within the prison system, and can last for months and years.

The well-respected international nongovernmental organization, Human Rights Watch, calls the use of control units in U.S. prisons a clear violation of human rights, and a breach of a United Nations treaty, the International Covenant on Civil and Political Rights, implemented in the United States in December 1992 after a 25-year delay ("Human Rights Violations," 1993).[2] In 1994, another group, International Prison Watch, wrote: "Cruel, inhuman or degrading treatment is commonplace in American prisons. Overcrowding and the growing tendency to segregate prisoners result in a frequent resort to punishment, above and beyond simple loss of liberty ("Detention Conditions," 1994, p. 136)."

California has three long-term disciplinary control units called Security Housing Units (SHU). Corcoran was opened in 1988 and houses 1,400 men. A year later the more infamous Pelican Bay facility began operation with 1,600 prisoners in an X-shaped windowless bunker. Women are not spared this measure of abuse. Valley State Prison for Women has its own SHU, which houses 52 women in solitary confinement. In the two years following the opening of the Pelican Bay SHU, prisoners filed more than 250 meritorious lawsuits alleging cruel and unusual punishment in violation of the Eighth Amendment of the U.S. Constitution. The presiding judge, Thelton Henderson of the Northern District Federal Court of California, had all individual claims combined into a single class action suit (*Madrid v. Gomez,* 1993). In her opening statement the attorney for the prisoners, Susan Creighton, stated, "The evidence will show that Pelican Bay was intended from the outset to inspire terror, intimidation, and dread. Brutality and terror are as much a part of the fabric of Pelican Bay as its gun tower and gate." Judge Henderson agreed with the prisoners and ruled in their favor in 1995 stating, "dry words on paper cannot adequately capture the senseless suffering and sometimes wretched misery that defendants' [prison staff and administration] unconstitutional practices leave in their wake."[3]

Putting gang-labeled prisoners in the SHU has been the centerpiece of California's strategy to deal with the serious problem of gang-run criminal activity and violence in its 33 prison facilities holding 156,000 men and women. Fifty percent of the prisoners in the SHUs are gang-labeled, and many have committed no serious rules violation other than being identified as a gang member by three pieces of information from confidential sources. This court of classification, where no defense can be mounted and no accuser can be faced, puts prisoners in the SHU under a "snitch, parole, or die" sentence. To exit the SHU, gang-labeled prisoners must inform on their alleged gang affiliates, leave prison on parole, or die. Thus many serve their entire sentence under SHU conditions because they took a picture on the yard with their homeboys, or had the phone number of a gang member in their address book, or were targeted by a snitch despite no true gang involvement. Certainly the prison administration must counter gang criminality. But using the SHU is a failed strategy. A former warden of a federal control unit testifying in the case criticized the placement of prison gang members in the SHU by saying, "Anybody who's been around prisons . . . knows you have to be [gang] affiliated or you have your head handed to you. My thesis is that gang members shouldn't be locked up, it's that violent people should be locked up."[4]

Gang activity continues unabated in California's prisons, and fighting among prisoners has been rising dramatically. California DOC statistics show that despite or possibly because of SHU punishment, between 1990 and 1995 inmate-inmate assaults rose almost three times faster than the growth rate of the prison population, while inmate-staff assaults grew at double the rate. Forensic psychiatrist Terry Kupers, MD, interviewed during a Human Rights Watch investigation of a control unit in Indiana, had this to say:

> A prisoner suffers panic attacks that began years ago when, as a new prisoner, he was dragged into a cell and raped by other prisoners. The panic reaches the point where he feels he has to cut himself to get some relief. The cutting does get him removed from his cell in solitary confinement in the SHU for a few hours respite in the infirmary while getting stitched up. But then he is returned to his cell and given an even longer SHU sentence for breaking the prison's rule against self-mutilation ("Cold Storage," 1997).

One expert on prison control units, Stuart Grassian, MD, described the situation in this way:[5]

> There is a notion in the popular mind that people who end up in solitary confinement are the most ruthless kind of James Cagneys of the prison system. In fact what you often see there is exactly the antithesis: they are very often the wretched of the earth, people who are mentally ill, illiterate, and cognitively impaired, people with neurological difficulties, people who just really can't manage to contain their behavior at times. The prison system tends to respond to this by punishment. Punishment tends to make their conditions worse and they tend to get into these vicious cycles where they continue to commit this disruptive behavior and they continue to go deeper and deeper into the belly of the prison system and get sicker and sicker. Solitary confinement itself can cause a very specific kind of psychiatric syndrome, which, in its worst stages can lead to an agitated, hallucinatory, confusional psychotic state often involving random violence and self-mutilation, suicidal behavior, a lot of real agitated, fearful and confusional kinds of symptoms.
>
> The problem is sooner or later they are going to get back into your community. And it's kind of like kicking and beating a dog and keeping it in a cage until it gets as crazy and vicious and wild as it can possibly get, and then one day you take it out

into the middle of the streets of San Francisco or Boston and you open the cage and you run away. That's no favor to the community.

Despite the obvious danger to the public, no studies have been done by the California Department of Corrections to track prisoners leaving its SHUs. However, a few notorious cases of murder and mayhem committed by recent releases have appeared in the press. One man, while drugged on speed, murdered a county sheriff's deputy, and another brutally raped a woman and threw her naked from his moving vehicle. Organizations doing relief work with the homeless report psychiatrically disabled parolees from the SHUs living on the streets in a confused and disorganized state.[6] Prisoners released from long-term SHU confinement describe problems with socialization and impulse control. Certainly such prisoners will be less able to get along and seek employment than when they went into prison, becoming a burden on families and communities already suffering from lack of resources, jobs, and social services.

The trauma of control units affects more than prisoners. Dr. Grassian described it in this way:[7]

> ... the really sobering fact is that the people who work in these settings day after day have seemed to lose their capacity to be shocked by the kinds of things that they see. There is a kind of brutalizing effect of the prison environment which, I think, makes everyone who is a part of it more sick, sicker . . . it makes the corrections officers sicker . . . It does tend to lead to a kind of brutalization, a kind of sadism. I was talking to some of the corrections officers and they were talking about what was happening to some of their friends—the rate of alcoholism had skyrocketed, spousal abuse, suicide. Working in that environment may put money in your pocket, but over time it destroys you psychologically and brings out rage and sadism and violence and brutality.

Despite being proven unconstitutionally brutal in Federal Court, Pelican Bay is not the most violent prison in California. The SHU at Corcoran Prison is where staff violence has reached its height. Under the "integrated yard policy," known enemies and rival groups were routinely mixed in the small group exercise yards (Weinstein, 1997).[8] Prisoners were used as pawns in these set-up fights for nine years. Guards promoted their champions and even bet on the fights for entertainment. It is estimated that 8,000 of these "gladiator fights" occurred between 1988 and 1997. By policy, guards used guns to control the yards. There were more than 2,000 shooting incidents at Corcoran, wounding hundreds and killing five prisoners. An independent analysis of the five lethal shootings showed that none was justified by the Department's own criteria, and that reports were falsified and sanitized in each case. Yet the "Shooting Review Board," routinely organized by the central prison administration, justified every shot ever fired on the Corcoran SHU yards. In a wrongful death lawsuit brought on behalf of the last prisoner gunned down on the yards, former California DOC Director Dan McCarthy testified that, "The rate of violence in the Corcoran SHU in its first year of operation was absolutely the highest rate I have ever seen in any institution anywhere in the country." Between 1989 and 1994 there were more than 2,500 shooting incidents in all of California prisons. Twenty-seven prisoners were killed. More prisoners were killed in California's prisons than in all other prisons in the United States combined.

None of this serves the citizens of California well. Brutality breeds hate, and hate breeds violence. Exposure to violence breeds violence. In an interview on the television news program, *60 Minutes* (January 15, 1995), reporter Mike Wallace asked Lt. Al Dienes, Pelican Bay's Information Officer, "Does Pelican Bay make society safer? Inmates, some actively psychotic, are regularly paroled directly from the Pelican Bay SHU to the street with no training, no counseling, no job and in many cases nowhere to go. How does society benefit, how does it lead to public safety?" Dienes could only say, "I can't answer your question, it's beyond us."

Notes

1. Interim Report by the Monitoring Project of the National Campaign to Stop Control Unit Prisons, 1997. Available from the American Friends Service Committee, 972 Broad Street, 6th Floor, Newark, NJ 07102.

2. Report available from International Prison Watch, 16 Avenue Berthelot, BP 67083, 69301 Lyon Cedex 07, France.

3. Findings of Fact, Conclusions of Law and Order, *Madrid v. Gomez* (1993).

4. Testimony of Charles Fenton in *Madrid v. Gomez* (1993).

5. "Psychological destruction due to isolation," published in *Survivors Manual: A Manual Written By and For People Living in Control Units.* (1997). Available from California Prison Focus, 2940 16th Street, San Francisco, CA 94103.

6. Reports to California Prison Focus, a human rights and advocacy group working with and for SHU prisoners.

7. From: *Survivors Manual: A Manual Written By and For People Living in Control Units.* (p. 61). 1997. (see note 4).

8. Information in this paragraph is from the personal knowledge of the author, gathered in the course of producing the video, *Maximum Security University*, which shows through prison surveillance tapes the killing of four prisoners at Corcoran by guard gunfire.

References

Cold storage: Super-maximum security confinement in Indiana. (1997). New York: Human Rights Watch.

Detention conditions for people in prison. (1994). France: International Prison Watch.

Human Rights Violations in the United States. (1993, December). New York: Human Rights Watch.

Madrid v. Gomez, No. C90-3094-THE, 9/17/93, US District Court for the Northern District of California.

Survivors manual: a manual written by and for people living in control units. (1997). San Francisco: California Prison Focus.

Weinstein, C. (Producer). (1997). *Maximum Security University* [video]. San Francisco: California Prison Focus.

21

Body and Soul
The Trauma of Prison Rape

Joanne Mariner

> *[Plaintiff L. T. is] a skinny, white, passive, non-violent, short timer, who is blind in his right eye. . . . [Upon arriving in prison], plaintiff was housed in the open barracks of number seven (7), which held about eighty (80) inmates. . . . Housed within seven (7) barracks were numerous types of characters without any regard for age v. youth, abled v. disabled, violent v. nonviolent, types of crimes, lengths of sentences, resulting in assaults, thefts, monetary and sexual pressures all of which plaintiff endured therein, and witnessed occurring to others. . . . On 1-25-97, at approximately 2:00 A.M., plaintiff went into the bathroom of seven (7) barracks and inmate C. Williams followed after. Plaintiff used the urinal and as he turned, inmate Williams pulled a shank (glass knife) from a book and threatened to poke plaintiffs other eye out and kill him if he did not let Williams fuck the plaintiff. Williams then told plaintiff to go to the rear corner of the bathroom, pulled a small bottle of lotion from his picket and made plaintiff rub it on his penis. Williams then put the shank to plaintiff's throat and said "turn around and pull those pants down," which plaintiff did for fear of his life if he did not. Williams then raped (penile penetration to anus) the plaintiff with the shank at plaintiff's throat, pressing it and say "shut up bitch" when plaintiff began to moan and want to scream from the pain. After climaxing and wiping himself off, Williams said "if you ever tell anyone, I or one of my gang members will kill you, in here or in the world."*[1]

L.T. is one of the many Americans who were raped in prison last year.[2] His experience of rape was, by his own account, violent, painful, and humiliating. Despite the mental trauma he suffered, he received no counseling following the incident, nor did he succeed in obtaining legal assistance in his subsequent court challenge to the abuse. Without having secured psychological treatment or any measure of accountability for the violent injustice he endured, he was paroled from prison this year.

It does not require a great deal of thought to anticipate the physical effects of prison rape—intense pain, abrasions, soreness, bleeding, and in some cases, tearing of the anus or transmission of the HIV virus—but its effects on the victim's psyche are much less evident. Based on correspondence and interviews with numerous inmates,[3] I am convinced that the psychological effects of prison rape are serious and enduring, and that they raise important questions regarding the failure of prison authorities to take effective measures to prevent such abuse. The physical brutality of rape is, of course, deplorable. Nonetheless, the physical impact of such abuse is likely to be less devastating, and far less permanent, than its psychological impact. Indeed, many instances of nonconsensual sex occur through coercion, threats, or deception: they may not leave any physical marks, only psychological injury.

As members of a society that incarcerates its citizens at one of the highest rates in the world,[4] Americans need to examine the larger consequences of these abuses. Inmates such as L.T., whether they fall victim to violent sexual attacks or to more subtle forms of sexual abuse, leave the prison system in a state of extreme psychological stress. Important questions arise as to how the trauma of sexual abuse resolves itself when inmates are released into society.

Paradoxically, the phenomenon of prison sexual abuse is both known and unknown, familiar and unfamiliar. Judging by the popular media, rape is accepted as almost a commonplace of imprisonment, so much so that when the topic of prison arises, a joking reference to rape seems almost obligatory. Few members of the public would be surprised by the assertion that men are frequently raped in prison, given rape's established place in the mythology of prison life. Yet, beyond the joking and snickering, serious discussion of the subject remains rare. Stephen Donaldson, late president of the organization Stop Prisoner Rape, once asserted that "the rape of males is a taboo subject for public discussion . . . If ever there was a crime hidden by a curtain of silence, it is male rape."[5] Indisputably, the hard facts about inmate-on-inmate sexual abuse are little known. Although the topic has been explored by various academics, the findings of different researchers are inconsistent, and in some instances, flatly contradictory.[6]

* * *

Prison reformers have a clear stake in asserting that prison abuses have a deleterious impact on the world outside of prisons, the logic being that even if the public cares not a whit for the suffering of inmate victims, everyone agrees on the desirability of preventing abuses against victims in the outside world. Not surprisingly, many reformers have asserted that stopping sexual abuse against prisoners is imperative for pragmatic as well as humanitarian reasons. According to this view, rape not only injures the victim's dignity and sense of self, it threatens to perpetuate a cycle of sexual violence. According to Stephen Donaldson:

> You take a guy who's been raped in prison and he is going to be filled with a tremendous amount of rage . . . Now eventually he is going to get out. Most people do. And all the studies show that today's victim is tomorrow's predator. So by refusing to deal with this in an intelligent way, you are genuinely sentencing society to an epidemic of future rapes.[7]

Donaldson's assertion that prison rape begets further crimes is not universally accepted. Daniel Lockwood, a criminologist who has written extensively on the topic of prison sexual violence, disputes the notion that victims of abuse, embittered by the experience, vent their hostility on the public when released from prison. He states there is "little reliable data" to support such claims, deriding the idea as a "damaging myth" (Lockwood, 1994, p. 99).

The dearth of longitudinal studies documenting the subsequent criminal history of victims of prison rape should not, however, put an end to all discussion of the topic. Obviously there is a need for further empirical research. Nonetheless, certain preliminary conclusions are possible.

First, it is clear that the effects of victimization are profound. Many victims of prison rape report continuing nightmares, deep depression, loss of self-esteem, self-hatred, and having considered or attempted suicide. The following account is typical:

> I have been getting sexually assaulted at [Prison X] by two inmates. I tried to commit suicide in hopes of relieving the misery of it. I was made to perform oral sex on the two inmates for exchange of protection from other inmates. I reported the action of the inmates to the Unit authority but did not get any help so that is when I slashed both my wrists in hope of dying.

Another prisoner told me:

> I did nine years from March 1983 to November 1991. In that nine years, I was raped several times. . . . I came back to prison in 1993. In 1994, I was raped again. I attempted suicide. . . . The doctor here in the prison say "quote" major depression multiple neurotic symptoms, marked by excessive fear, unrelenting worry and debilitating anxiety. Antisocial suicidal ideation, self-degradation, paranoia and hopelessness are characteristic, "unquote."[8]

In addition to general feelings of fear, depression, and self-hatred, many prisoners have expressed a more specific anxiety about the loss of gender identity, fearing that their "manhood" has been damaged or eroded. As one sexually abused prisoner confessed, "I feel that maybe some women might look at me as less than a man. My pride feels beaten to a pulp."[9] Inmates speak of other raped prisoners as being "converted to women," or "made into homosexuals" as if one's sexuality might be irretrievably altered by the fact of rape.

The belief that rape damages one's innermost self is strong among inmates. Indeed, for the perpetrators of rape, this belief provides a compelling reason to commit the act: rape appears to be the most powerful way to injure and degrade its victims. But what comes of the victims' conviction that they have been fundamentally damaged? My research suggests that at least some minority of prisoners who endure sexual abuse will turn to violence.

James Gilligan, in his theory of violence, argues that shame is the primary underlying cause of the problem (Gilligan, 1996). Driven by shame, men murder, rape, and punish others. In describing prisons as fertile territory for the shame-violence relationship, Gilligan's observations are consistent with prisoners' reports of their experiences. As one inmate told me, "When I came out of prison, I remember thinking that others knew I had been raped just by looking at me. My behavior changed to such cold heartedness that I resented anyone who found reason to smile, to laugh, and to be happy."[10] This man later committed rape after release from prison in what he said was a kind of revenge on the world.

Another inmate explained the dynamic in the following way:

> It's fixed where if you're raped, the only way you [can escape further abuse is if] you rape someone else. Yes I know that's fully screwed, but that's how your head is twisted. After it's over you may be disgusted with yourself, but you realize you're not powerless and that you can deliver as well as receive pain. Then it's up to you to decide whether you enjoy it or not. Most do, I don't.[11]

Beyond encouraging violent behavior from its victims, prison rape also evokes violence from prisoners not directly exposed to it. Many inmates, including those who are relatively nonviolent by nature, resort to violence as a protective shield against rape, to prove that they are not to be bullied. Studies have found that even the vague, indeterminate possibility of rape is a powerful impetus for prison violence.

Interestingly, even though violent behavior in prison constitutes a disciplinary infraction and can, in serious cases, result in criminal prosecution and more prison time, corrections officials frequently urge inmates to employ violence to defend themselves from attack. Lockwood, among others, has reported that prisoners are counseled by prison staff to respond to the threat of sexual assault by fighting the aggressor (Lockwood, 1980, pp. 53-54). Inmates have often told me that guards warn them, "no one is going to baby sit you," letting them know that they have to "act like a man," that is, to react violently to aggressive sexual overtures.

It seems unlikely that such violence—even though it is spawned, nurtured, and grown in the correctional setting—will remain locked in prison when the inmates leave.

* * *

It might be assumed that some victims of prison rape would find a degree of solace in securing accountability for the abuses committed against them—in knowing that the rapists have been suitably punished, and that prison authorities have been forced to acknowledge their negligence in failing to prevent the abuse. Unfortunately, our justice system offers scant relief to sexually abused prisoners. Few public prosecutors are concerned with prosecuting crimes committed against inmates, preferring to leave internal prison problems to the discretion of the prison authorities. Similarly, prison officials themselves rarely refer prisoner-on-prisoner abuses out for prosecution. As a result, perpetrators of prison rape almost never face criminal charges.

Internal disciplinary mechanisms, the putative substitute for criminal prosecution, also tend to function poorly in the relatively rare cases in which the victim reports the crime. In nearly every instance I've encountered, the authorities have imposed light disciplinary sanctions against the perpetrator—perhaps 30 days in disciplinary segregation—if that. Often rapists are simply transferred to another facility, or are not moved at all. Their victims, in contrast, may be forced to spend the rest of their prison terms in protective custody, where conditions are generally the equivalent of disciplinary segregation: 23 hours per day in a small cell, no privileges, no TV, restricted phone calls. Such is the topsy-turvy world of prisons, where the victims may be punished instead of the perpetrators.

Disappointingly, many federal judges respond with extreme callousness to claims of prison abuse. Despite the paucity of lawyers willing to litigate such cases, some inmates do nonetheless file suit against the prison authorities in the aftermath of rape, claiming that the authorities' failure to take steps to protect them from abuse violates the Eighth Amendment. All too often, such cases are dismissed in the early stages of litigation, with judges going out of their way to excuse the actions of prison officials. Moreover, the rare case that does survive summary judgment and finally reaches a jury typically finds the inmate plaintiff before an audience that is wholly unreceptive to his story: one that sympathizes with the prison authorities rather than with the "criminal."[12] Although there have been a few generous damage awards in prison rape cases, they are the very rare exceptions to the rule.

22

Feeding a Public Health Epidemic

John P. May

Figure 22.1 A jail routine in Chicago.

Photograph by Lloyd DeGreen. Reprinted with permission.

In the early 1990s, the Centers for Disease Control reported outbreaks of an infectious disease in several New York hospitals. Many patients, including state prison inmates, were infected and were not responding to the usual medications. Before the outbreak was fully recognized, several inmates had been transported throughout the state and had unknowingly spread the disease. Doctors eventually determined the illness to be a strain of tuberculosis resistant to all available medications. Before the outbreak could be controlled, at least 42 inmates developed this strain of tuberculosis, 84% of whom died within 12 months. One correctional officer also died from the outbreak. Another officer infected his young son before diagnosis (Greifinger, Heywood, & Glaser, 1993; Valway, Greifinger, et al., 1994; Valway, Richards, et al., 1994). At the same time, different prison hospital systems across the country began reporting their own cases of drug-resistant tuberculosis.

At the peak of this outbreak, state correctional facilities were nearly one quarter over their designed capacity, and federal facilities were nearly half over capacity. It was widely acknowledged that prison overcrowding facilitated the spread of this deadly disease. The Centers for Disease Control responded by launching new offensives against this new form of tuberculosis, including close attention to correctional facilities, while federal court orders and consent decrees specified conditions related to overcrowding in one of every seven state correctional facilities (U.S. Dept. of Health & Human Services, 1995, pp. 9-10).

The transmission of drug-resistant tuberculosis within prison systems is just one example of the inescapable connection between public health and incarcerated populations. Several other examples have appeared in recent years. In Houston, strains of drug-resistant pneumococcal pneumonia emerged in an overcrowded and poorly ventilated jail (Hoge et al., 1994). In Los Angeles, an outbreak of meningitis in the city jail moved into the surrounding neighborhoods (Tappero et al., 1996). Infectious diseases such as HIV, hepatitis, and other sexually transmitted diseases are common in jails and prisons, and eventually make their way to the streets.

Just as infectious diseases can flourish in and emerge from jails and prisons, so can violence. It is well known that specific acts of violence such as gang hits or assassinations have been orchestrated behind prison walls and played out in the streets. But beyond such outright events, the violence that prison breeds spills out in the community in other ways. Attitudes, behaviors, and lessons learned by inmates and staff in prison are transmitted into the free society during incarceration, upon release, or when home from work. Most prisoners have a network of family and associates who are also affected by their incarceration and share it with them. As they leave prison, the culture of prison flows into the streets with them through clothing, music, slang, and possibly old or unsettled scores.

Each year in the United States, incredibly, more than 10 million people are released from jail or prison (Jankowski, 1992, table 2.4). Few other experiences are shared by such a large segment of the population. If incarceration was successful in rehabilitating individuals, such mass movements of the population might be of benefit to the society as is, for example, the yearly graduation of nearly two million people from colleges and universities (U.S. Bureau of the Census, 1995, table 303). Or, if there was a vaccine to protect against violence, and this could be given to each inmate upon leaving the institution, the diffusion effect into the community would be very beneficial. In reality, however, the community rarely benefits.

Prisons are violent places, and prisons teach violence. Anyone walking into a prison for the first time can feel the tension. The concrete and steel walls and floors serve to echo and intensify the noises of chains, steel doors slamming, yelling, cursing, and beatings. For an inmate who must make the prison his or her home, whether for months, years, or even a lifetime, avoiding a violent attack becomes a daily concern. The need to maintain constant vigilance creates stress, tension, and chronic anxiety. Even in their sleep, they do not feel safe. They almost instinctively react to provocation with violence, as adjustment to this sense of vulnerability.

Fights and stabbings occur daily in correctional institutions. Fortunately, homicides are few, mostly a testament to the absence of firearms and the proximity of response teams. Nevertheless, prison culture teaches inmates to "toughen up" in order to make it. They learn to solve conflicts through force.

Jails and prisons also teach *control* as a means to achieving ends. Inmates are controlled almost every minute by correctional staff, legislators, and fellow inmates. This control is most often achieved through aggression, power, strength, and intimidation. Inmates become conditioned to these modes of behavior and operation, but if they apply them on the streets they find trouble.

This is, in fact, what happens. The largest study of persons released from prisons found that 62.5% were rearrested for a felony or serious misdemeanor within three years, including 22.7% rearrested for violent offenses. Nearly one fifth of those who had been imprisoned for nonviolent offenses were rearrested for violent offenses. The strongest predictor of recidivism was a prior arrest before the most recent incarceration. Such persons were nearly 20% more likely to be rearrested than those who had been incarcerated only once (Beck & Shipley, 1989). In another study of nearly 3,000 juvenile offenders in Florida, those sent to an adult prison were much more likely to be rearrested than youth not sent to an adult prison, even though they were matched for similar original offenses (Bishop, Frazier, Lanza-Kaduce, & Winner, 1996). In short, studies find that those most frequently or intensely exposed to prison environments are the ones most likely to reoffend.

That prisons generate violence is further demonstrated by the phenomenon that many parolees become victims of violence. When people are released from prison and jail, their risk of a violent death increases dramatically. Parolees have a death rate at least fourfold higher than their non-incarcerated peers (May, 1998). Homicide is the single leading cause of premature death for young persons paroled from prison. (Many also die prematurely from car crashes or HIV—also consequences of high-risk behaviors.) A study of nearly 4,000 teenagers paroled from the California Youth Authority during the 1980s found that 181 died within 10 years of parole, 54% from homicide. The rate of homicide for this group was more than fivefold higher than for similar youth matched within the same high-risk age and race group. In another study, the Illinois Department of Corrections found that homicide was the cause of death for 50% of their parolee deaths during the 1980s. Studies have shown, in fact, that many homicide victims have had prior involvement with the criminal justice system (Chicago Police Department, 1993; Dawson & Boland, 1993; McGonigal et al., 1993). It seems that the risk factors for becoming a victim of homicide follow the same patterns as those for becoming a perpetrator (Block & Christakos, 1995).

Many prisoners grew up in violent environments, witnessed brutal acts of violence, and have themselves been victims of violence. A study in the Cook County Jail in Chicago found that one in four men entering had been shot at least once in his life (May, Ferguson, Ferguson, & Cronin, 1995), and the same frequency was found among men entering the Washington, D.C. jail. One third still carried the bullets in their bodies (May, Pitts, & Oen, 1997). Many female inmates have been victims of domestic battery, and one third have been victims of childhood sexual or physical abuse (Snell & Morton, 1994). The prison experience does little to heal these wounds; rather, it tolerates or reinforces violence.

As it turns out, involvement in the criminal justice system may be the single best predictor of the probability that a person will be injured or killed through violence, or later perpetrate violence (Rosenfeld & Decker, 1993). As an example of victimization risk, a study of adolescents in Richmond, Virginia, found that kids in the juvenile justice system were 22 times more likely to have been shot than kids not in the system, and their first arrest preceded the injury in 90% of the cases (McLaughlin et al., 1996). As an example of perpetration risk, a study of multiple urban areas found that three fourths of murderers had prior arrests (Dawson & Boland, 1993).

Something happens (or does not happen in the way of rehabilitation) within jails or prisons that increases a person's risk for either violent death or perpetration upon release. The reason for the increased risk has never been determined or studied, but it is a clear signal that something is wrong. It is not only by chance that parolees die prematurely or perpetrate violence in far greater numbers than peers who do not have prison experiences.

Violence behaves as a contagious disease. It is most often clustered in particular areas, increasing over time, and escalating from person to person (Loftin, 1986)—making prisons fertile ground for violence. Given the extraordinary history of victimization among the incarcerated and the absence of a therapeutic environment, violence is predictable. As prisons become more crowded, inmates serve more time, and more people flow through the system, the spread of their violence is inevitable. As learned with tuberculosis, epidemics in jails and prisons can be ignored only at the peril of the community.

References

Beck, A. J., & Shipley, B. E. (1989). *Recidivism of prisoners released in 1983*. Bureau of Justice Statistics special report (NCJ-116261). Washington, DC: U.S. Department of Justice.

Bishop, D. M., Frazier, C. E., Lanza-Kaduce, L., & Winner, L. (1996). The transfer of juveniles to criminal court: Does it make a difference? *Crime and Delinquency, 42*(2), 171-191.

Block, C. R., & Christakos, A. (1995). Chicago homicide from the sixties to the nineties: Major trends in lethal violence. In *Proceedings of the Third Annual Spring Symposium of the Homicide Research Working Group* (pp. 17-50). NCJ-154254. Washington, DC: National Institute of Justice.

Chicago Police Department. (1993). *Murder analysis*. Detective Division internal report.

Dawson, J. M., & Boland, B. (1993). *Murder in large urban counties, 1988*. Bureau of Justice Statistics special report (NCJ-140614). Washington, DC: U.S. Department of Justice.

Greifinger, R. B., Heywood, N. J., & Glaser, J. B. (1993). Tuberculosis in prison: balancing justice and public health. *Journal of Law, Medicine and Ethics, 21*(3-4), 332-341.

Hoge, C. W., Reichler, M. R., Dominguez, E. A., Bremer, J. C., Mastro, T. D., Hendricks, K. A., Musher, D. M., Elliott, J. A., Facklam, R. R., & Breiman, R. F. (1994). An epidemic of pneumococcal disease in an overcrowded, inadequately ventilated jail. *New England Journal of Medicine, 331*(10), 643-648.

Jankowski, C. W. (1992). *Correctional populations in the United States, 1990*. Washington, DC: Office of Justice Programs, Bureau of Justice Statistics, U.S. Department of Justice.

Loftin, C. (1986). Assaultive violence as a contagious social process. *Bulletin of the New York Academy of Medicine, 62*(5), 550-555.

May, J. P. (1998). Preventive health issues for individuals in jails and prison. In M. Puisis (Ed.), *Correctional health care*. St. Louis, MO: Mosby Publishing.

May, J. P., Ferguson, M. G., Ferguson, R., & Cronin, K. (1995). Prior nonfatal firearm injuries in detainees of a large urban jail. *Journal of Health Care for the Poor and Underserved, 6*(2), 162-176.

May, J. P., Pitts, K., & Oen, R. (1997, November). *Responding to the patient with a gunshot wound.* Presentation to the National Commission on Correctional Health Care (Chicago), San Antonio, TX.

McGonigal, M. D., Cole, J., Schwab, C. W., Kauder, D. R., Rotondo, M. F., & Angood, P. B. (1993). Urban firearm deaths: A five-year perspective. *Journal of Trauma, 35*(4), 532-537.

McLaughlin, C. R., Reiner, S. M., Waite, D. E., Reams, P. N., Joost, T. F., Anderson, J. L., & Gervin, A. S. (1996, November). *Firearm injuries in juvenile offenders: A public health crisis.* Abstract presented to the 124th annual meeting of the American Public Health Association, New York, NY.

Rosenfeld, R., & Decker, S. (1993). Where public health and law enforcement meet: Monitoring and preventing youth violence. *American Journal of Police, 12*(3), 11-57.

Snell, T. L., & Morton, D. (1994). *Women in prison.* Bureau of Justice Statistics special report (NCJ-145321). Washington, DC: U.S. Department of Justice.

Tappero, J. W., Reporter, R., Wenger, J. D., Ward, B. A., Reeves, M. W., Missbach, T. S., Plikaytis, B. D., Mascola, L., & Schuchat, A. (1996). Meningococcal disease in Los Angeles County, California, and among men in the county jails. *New England Journal of Medicine, 335*(12), 833-840.

U.S. Bureau of the Census. (1995). *Statistical abstract of the United States: 1995* (115th edition). Washington, DC: Government Printing Office.

U.S. Dept. of Health and Human Services. (1995). *Controlling TB in correctional facilities.* Atlanta, GA: Centers for Disease Control.

Valway, S. E., Greifinger, R. B., Papania, M., Kilburn, J. O., Woodley, C., DiFerdinando, G. T., & Dooley, S. W. (1994). Multidrug-resistant tuberculosis in the New York State prison system, 1990-1991. *Journal of Infectious Diseases, 170,* 151-156.

Valway, S. E., Richards, S. B., Kovacovich, J., Greifinger, R. B., Crawford, J. T., & Dooley, S. W. (1994). Outbreak of multi-drug-resistant tuberculosis in a New York State prison, 1991. *American Journal of Epidemiology, 140,* 113-122.

23

Violence and Incarceration
A Personal Observation

JoAnne Page

Violence is a dominant and defining thread running through the fabric of jail and prison life. It shapes the culture of the institution and the fears, behaviors, and values of the prisoners within the walls. The violence of the jail and prison world is often a reinforcement of violence in the lives of prisoners who were abused as children and grew up on streets where their lives were not safe or valued by the larger society. The culture of violence, whether it is reinforced or learned for the first time in jail and prison, leaves the institution walls in the souls and the internal scar tissue of prisoners upon their release, and is brought home with them to their families and communities.

Norwegian criminologist Nils Christie has described prisons as factories of pain; just as societies are careful about how much money they put into circulation, they should be equally careful about how much pain they choose to circulate. Jails and prisons are also factories and catalysts of violence. The United States is decades into an experiment of escalating incarceration, striking in the extent of its reach into the fabric of the lives of its citizens and its communities. Its profound consequences in terms of individual and community impact upon generations, civil liberties, and use of resources are simply not discussed enough as incarceration continues to grow. The time for such a discussion is now.

For 25 years, I have had experience in jails and prisons and with released prisoners. I have many stories from inside and outside correctional walls, many of which reflect the insidious damage of prison culture. One of my first experiences occurred at the Green Haven Correctional Facility in New York, I learned that one of the quiet, male offenders in my group had been the victim of a prison gang rape. I was stunned by the information, but even more by the casual way in which it was conveyed and the way he was treated by other members of the group. He was disrespected, shunned, and harassed. The other prisoners viewed the rape as his fault because he was unable to effectively defend himself. The blame that he received hit me harder than the fact of the rape itself.

I went home that night and asked my father, a concentration camp survivor, for an explanation, having previously used his experience as a way of understanding the culture of confinement. He told me that, in the concentration camp, the weak were feared and seen as a danger to the survival of others. Having grown up in a culture that protected weakness, I had stepped into a culture in which weakness was a crime punishable by violence up to and including death. I never forgot that first harsh awakening into the reality of the world I was visiting.

Other stories are worth sharing. I remember sitting in the back of a car driven by several ex-offenders and hearing them talk about their friend who had just been released. He was locked up again on a homicide charge, "gotten for a body" they related matter-of-factly. While I was teaching one of my prison classes, an extremely polite student came in late. He apologized profusely for his lateness, explaining that someone had been stabbed on his prison tier and it had taken a while to mop up the mess. It was clear from his explanation that the stabbing was troubling and worthy of note only because it had made him late.

I remember teaching another class deep within Sing Sing prison and discovering that most of my students were carrying knives because stabbings regularly occurred in the corridor through which they had to pass on the way to class. I walked into Green Haven one day and heard allegations that an inmate patient had been beaten to death by correction officers. I tried to conduct business as usual while the ex-offenders with me collected personal statements from prisoners who were jeopardizing their own safety by coming forward about the details. I remember their rage and sense of helplessness at the end of the day but, even more, I remember their shock that I still had the capacity to be surprised at such a killing.

Prison stories blend with stories I have heard from ex-offenders after their release. One man who had served almost 20 years described what it was like for him to step into a subway and be shoved by another rider. He began swinging to attack in an automatic move that he learned behind bars, only to stop short upon seeing that the person who had shoved him was a little old lady with shopping bags. Had the person been male and anywhere near his age, violence would have resulted, and he would have viewed his actions as self-defensive, based on the conduct code he had learned behind bars. Another man, also released after many years, described to me how he was walking down the street and heard running footsteps behind him. Swinging around to attack or defend, he saw a jogger coming at him and put his fists down in embarrassment.

It is natural, upon release, to bring the culture of prison to the street. It is easy, translating through a prison context, to see behavior that is innocent within the larger society as requiring self-defense through attack.

I have spent many years working with people behind bars. I have seen the profound lessons that incarceration teaches and reinforces. The lessons include an ability to shut off emotion, the definition of weakness as a justification for violence and exploitation, the casualness with which violence is regarded as a daily part of living, and a culture in which preemptive full-force attack is a necessary means of self-defense when hostility is anticipated. Triggers for such anticipation can include the pushing, staring, and rude comments that are part of the pattern of daily urban life. Incarceration also breeds and fosters "global rage," an impulsive and explosive anger so great that a minor incident can trigger an uncontrolled response.

I have seen the struggle of those who have been socialized to prison life as they attempt the difficult transition from a world of criminals, violence, and incarceration to a world of wage earners, caring families, and a free society. I have seen how the values and life skills learned while incarcerated, and the accumulated pain and rage, jeopardize such a transition. They are further handicapped if the communities to which they return are saturated with violence, drugs, and poverty. Often the slide back into the destructive and violent street world, and eventual reincarceration or death, is the path of least resistance. The way out of the cycle of crime and incarceration is uphill, and all too many cannot break out of the pattern that they have learned so well.

After 25 years of working in jails and prisons, and with ex-offenders who have survived them, there are some things I know. I know that people have a powerful will toward health and hope, and I have seen that will used to transform lives that looked damaged and destructive beyond salvaging. I have had the extraordinary privilege of being able to witness and support such transformation. I have heard my prisoner students say that, in growing up, they saw their future options as dying or being locked up. I know that it is a terrible crime at an unacceptable cost to allow so many young people to grow up with such a bleak sense of the future.

There are things that I do not know, and they scare me. I do not know what the United States will become as it continues locking up more and more of its young people. Certainly not the "land of the free." I do not know what happens to the soul and the future of communities most hard-hit by incarceration, communities that see their young people achieve their formative acculturation in handcuffs and behind bars. Or what happens when states spend more money on incarceration than on education. Or what the children of the women being incarcerated in record numbers will look like in 10 years. Or whether the casualty rate among young black men will keep escalating.

For 25 years I have worked with people doing time in prisons and jails. I have seen the anger and destructiveness that these institutions breed and foster. We live in a very small world; our lives are connected by a fragile and intimate weave. We are increasingly choosing to build factories of rage and pain and violence. We are choosing to destroy lives and communities, to plant dragon seeds. And if there is any lesson that we know, it is that we reap what we sow.

For this latter theory to hold, each of the following must be true: 1) employers must consider the criminal history records of ex-offenders when hiring; 2) the employer response to criminal history records must lead to an increase in job instability, over and above what would have occurred in the absence of any employer reaction; and 3) the increase in job instability caused by the "stigma" of arrest, conviction, and/or incarceration must cause an individual to commit crimes. Although no study has examined these components together, each individual component has been studied in some detail.

The first point is the most obvious and easiest to establish. By way of definition, labeling theory in criminology predicts that formal labels from social agents in the criminal justice system can "type" or "cast" an individual as "essentially" deviant, even if the individual is otherwise nondeviant (Garfinkel, 1956; Lemert, 1951; Matza, 1969; Scheff, 1966; Scott, 1972). The consequence of being typed as essentially deviant is that, in the eyes of others, one becomes generally less trustworthy and is seen as one who "might break other important rules." An employer who uses the existence of a criminal history record to exclude an individual from consideration for a job, without consideration of the applicant's other merits, would effectively be labeling an individual in the manner described above.[3]

The evidence suggests that employers do in fact make use of criminal history records in the manner described above. According to a survey by Hulsey (1990), employers who will not hire ex-offenders are most concerned about the general "trustworthiness" of the ex-offender rather than anything specifically related to the offense or the job in question. In addition, federal legislation explicitly denies ex-felons employment in *any* job in the financial sector, as well as in other areas such as child care and private investigation. Most states also have legislation mandating screening on the basis of criminal history records for literally hundreds of jobs, either directly or through licensing requirements for "good moral character." Survey evidence also demonstrates that employers sometimes refuse employment to an individual solely on the basis of his criminal history record. Perhaps the best known study was conducted by Schwartz and Skolnick (1964), who found that job applications of convicted individuals faced a statistically significant lower probability of generating a positive response than did the applications of non-offenders. More recently, an employer survey in five major U.S. cities for relatively unskilled jobs found that roughly 65% of all employers would not knowingly hire an ex-offender (regardless of the offense), and between 30% and 40% actually checked the criminal history records of their most recently hired employee (Holzer, 1996). Although some authors (Belair, 1988) question whether or not employers in fact base employment decisions on criminal history records, the evidence seems overwhelming in favor of the conclusion that criminal history records matter to at least some employers.

Having established the first point, it becomes important to consider the second point—we need to establish that labeling results in significant job instability over and above what would otherwise occur. The latter part of the statement is important—the existence of a relationship between unemployment and crime is unquestioned, but the causal mechanism is unclear. For example, a delinquent youth might have problems maintaining stable employment absent any action by employers, because of individual characteristics such as low intelligence or low self-control which contribute to both poor employment outcomes and criminal activity (Gottfredson & Hirschi, 1990). Or, if Hagan (1993) is correct, individuals can become embedded in a criminal activity. Because of their involvement in crime, they develop poor job skills and limited social networks, which in turn sharply limit their ability to find or succeed in "good" jobs. Therefore, studies need to establish that the permanent criminal history record causes the employment problems. To do this, researchers control both for individual characteristics that could cause criminal activity and poor employment outcomes, and for criminal activity itself. This can be done with longitudinal data sets that include multiple observations of both criminal activity and official sanctions over time.

Although many studies look at this issue, only six studies meet these criteria at some level. Of these, only one, by Hagan (1993), found that conviction had no effect on job instability. The remaining five found that arrest, conviction, or incarceration decrease job stability by between 6% and 30% for American and British youth, with the size of the effect apparently depending in part on the severity of the contact with the criminal justice system (Bushway, 1998; Freeman, 1991; Nagin & Waldfogel, 1995; Sampson & Laub, 1993).

These results suggest that employer "discrimination" against ex-offenders can lead to problems in the labor market, but the third and most important link still remains to be established: that job instability causes crime. Initial research using aggregate data found inconsistent results, but the general pattern was a weak positive relationship between unemployment and crime rates (Chiricos, 1987; Freeman, 1995).

Subsequent studies concentrated on individual level data. These studies routinely found that criminals are disproportionately members of demographic groups with low (and decreasing) employment potential, such as young men with limited education who score poorly on standardized tests. Furthermore, these studies established without question that incarcerated offenders were more likely to have troubled job histories and lower incomes than their counterparts (Freeman, 1987; Tauchen, Dryden, & Griesinger, 1994).

Once again, however, these types of correlations do not prove that unemployment causes crime. Additional factors like low intelligence and low self-control could cause both high unemployment and high crime. Furthermore, people who participate in crime can choose to be unemployed, in order to pursue their criminal activities. Therefore, studies that control for individual differences while establishing that crime occurred during periods of job instability are needed. There are two studies that appear to do this. Farrington, Gallagher, Morley, St. Ledger, and West (1986) found that crime increased during spells of unemployment for those youth who were predisposed toward crime. In contrast, Horney, Osgood, and Marshall (1995) found that employment status did not predict offending behavior for a month-to-month (retrospective) sample of convicted felons.

One possible explanation for the conflicting nature of these results is that the measures do not capture the key crime prevention components of the employment relationship. Rather than thinking about the causal structure only in terms of money, Sampson and Laub (1997) contend that the anti-criminogenic nature of work comes from the social bonds formed in some types of work environments. Individuals committed to and involved in their work are less likely to jeopardize these bonds with criminal activity. There is evidence that attachment to work and job stability make up the second strongest predictor of resistance, behind marriage. Crutchfield and Pitchford (1997) suggest that job quality will also affect an individual's decision to commit a crime. They found that people involved in short-term "dead-end" jobs are more likely to commit crimes than people in long-term jobs. Although attachment to work and job quality are not typically included in studies of the relationship between unemployment and crime, they might yield useful information when studied.

Although the idea that incarceration might lead to increased crime by creating job instability is no longer particularly popular in policy circles, there is evidence in academic research that employer discrimination does lead to job instability, and that job instability can lead to increased crime. This latter fact is the weak link in the causal structure. It should be clear from the work already done that the causal mechanism is more complicated than the "poor people commit crime for money" mechanism originally imagined 30 years ago when the idea first became popular. Nonetheless, employment challenges for the ex-offender are plentiful.

Notes

1. This chapter focuses generally on ex-offenders (individuals who have been convicted), rather than solely on individuals who have been incarcerated.

2. Also, states often limited access to public employment and allowed licensing boards to use ex-offender status as evidence against the "good moral character" requirement embedded in many licensing requirements.

3. Not all uses of a criminal history record by employers can be accurately described as labeling. Employers can make use of criminal history information as a *sig-*

nal in a relative assessment of an individual's job qualifications. Examples of cases in which employers would interpret a criminal history record as a *signal* rather than a *label* include restricting convicted drunk drivers from jobs as truck drivers, or restricting an individual arrested multiple times (but not convicted) for child molestation from working in a child care center.

References

Baker, S., & Sadd, S. (1981). *Diversion of felony arrests: An experiment in pretrial intervention: An evaluation of the court employment project, summary report.* Washington, DC: U.S. Department of Justice, National Institute of Justice.

Belair, R. (1988). *Public access to criminal history record information.* NCJ-111458. Prepared by SEARCH Group, Inc., for Criminal Justice Information Policy series, Bureau of Justice Statistics. Washington, DC: U.S. Department of Justice.

Bushway, S. (1997). *Labor-market effects of permitting employer access to criminal history records.* Working paper. University of Maryland, Department of Criminology.

Bushway, S. (1998). The impact of an arrest on the job stability of young white American men. *Journal of Research in Crime and Delinquency, 35*(4), 454-479.

Bushway, S., & Reuter, P. (1997). Review of labor market crime prevention programs. In L. W. Sherman, D. Gottfredson, D. MacKenzie, J. Eck, P. Reuter, & S. Bushway (Eds.), *Preventing crime: What works, what doesn't, what's promising* (NCJ 165366). Washington, DC: U.S. Department of Justice, Office of Justice Programs, National Institute of Justice.

Chiricos, T. (1987). Rates of crime and unemployment: An analysis of aggregate research evidence. *Social Problems, 34,* 187-212.

Cook, P. (1975). The correctional carrot: Better jobs for parolees. *Policy Analysis, 1,* 11-51.

Crutchfield, R., & Pitchford, S. (1997). Work and crime: The effects of labor stratification. *Social Forces, 76*(1), 93-118.

Downing, D. (1985). *Employer biases toward the hiring and placement of male ex-offenders.* Unpublished dissertation, Southern Illinois University at Carbondale.

Farrington, D., Gallagher, B., Morley, L., St. Ledger, R., & West, D. (1986). Unemployment, school leaving, and crime. *British Journal of Criminology, 26* (4), 335-356.

Freeman, R. (1987, Summer/Fall). The relation of criminal activity to black youth employment. *Review of Black Political Economy,* 99-107.

Freeman, R. (1991). *Crime and the employment of disadvantaged youth.* National Bureau of Economic Research working paper. Cambridge, MA: Harvard University.

Freeman, R. (1995). The labor market. In J. Q. Wilson & J. Petersilia (Eds.), *Crime.* San Francisco: Institute for Contemporary Studies.

Garfinkel, H. (1956). Conditions of successful degradation ceremonies. *American Journal of Sociology, 6,* 420-424.

Gottfredson, M., & Hirschi, T. (1990). *A general theory of crime.* Stanford, CA: Stanford University Press.

Hagan, J. (1993). The social embeddedness of crime and unemployment. *Criminology*, *31*, 465-492.

Holzer, H. (1996). *What employers want: Job prospects for less-educated workers.* New York: Russell Sage.

Horney, J., Osgood, D., & Marshall, I. (1995). Criminal careers in the short-term: Intra-individual variability in crime and its relation to local life circumstances. *American Sociological Review, 60*, 655-673.

Hulsey, L. (1990). *Attitudes of employers with respect to hiring released prisoners.* Unpublished dissertation, Mankato State University.

Lemert, E. (1951). *Social pathology.* New York: McGraw-Hill.

Martinson, R. (1974). What works? Questions and answers about prison reform. *The Public Interest, 35*, 25-27.

Matza, D. (1969). *Becoming deviant.* Englewood Cliffs, NJ: Prentice Hall.

Miller, N. (1979). *Employer barriers to the employment of persons with records of arrest or conviction: A review and analysis* (ASPER Report No. PUR-79 3204 A). Washington, DC: U.S. Department of Labor, ASPER.

Nagin, D., & Waldfogel, J. (1995). The effects of criminality and conviction on the labor market status of young British offenders. *International Review of Law and Economics, 15*, 109-126.

Paul v. Davis, 424, U.S. 693 (1976).

Robins, L. (1966). *Deviant children grown up.* Baltimore: Williams and Wilkins.

Rossi, P., Berk, R., & Lenihan, K. (1980). *Money, work, and crime: Experimental evidence.* New York: Academic Press.

Sampson, R., & Laub, J. (1993). *Crime in the making: Pathways and turning points through life.* Cambridge, MA: Harvard University Press.

Sampson, R., & Laub, J. (1997). A life-course theory of cumulative disadvantage and the stability of delinquency. In T. Thornberry (Ed.), *Developmental theories of crime and delinquency.* New Brunswick, NJ: Transaction Publishing.

Scheff, T. (1966). *Being mentally ill.* Chicago: Aldine.

Schwartz, R., & Skolnick, J. (1964). Two studies of legal stigma. In H. S. Becker (Ed.), *The other side: Perspectives of deviance.* New York: Free Press.

Scott, R. (1972). A proposed framework for analyzing deviance as a property of social order. In R. Scott & J. Douglas (Eds.), *Theoretical perspectives on deviance.* New York: Basic Books.

SEARCH. (1988). *Technical Report No. 13: Standards for the security and privacy of criminal history record information* (3rd ed.). Sacramento, CA: Author.

Tauchen, H., Dryden, A., & Griesinger, H. (1994). Criminal deterrence: Revisiting the issue with a birth cohort. *Review of Economics and Statistics, 76*(3), 399-412.

Thornberry, T. (1987). Toward an interactional theory of delinquency." *Criminology, 25*, 863-891.

25

A Prisoner's Journey

Randy Blackburn, ID#B-54426

The American criminal justice system is a business industry that is on the rise every day. Its primary function is to help politicians. It does not help those who are or have been incarcerated. Our government officials might tell the American people that the system rehabilitates people, but this is not true. The only people rehabilitated are those who rehabilitate themselves.

Once a person has been convicted of a crime, there is no help. Some prisons have programs that might help a person, but attendance is usually not mandatory. Often the programs are too limited and a person couldn't get in one if he wanted to. From my perspective, justice does not work, in or out of prison.

I speak of these things because I experienced the American criminal justice system first hand. On December 11, 1992, I was arrested for sexual assault on a nine-year-old girl. Although I told the officials that I was innocent, the State's Attorney, for unknown reasons, would not allow my witnesses to testify. I spent five years in prison for a crime that I did not commit.

My girlfriend and I were babysitting for a friend's three children: two girls and one boy. I was accused of fondling one of the girls. The kids were together in the front room sleeping, and my girlfriend and I were asleep in our bedroom for the entire evening. The girl in the middle later told her mother that I touched her vagina. It was an outrageous and completely untrue accusation.

Before court, my girlfriend pleaded to the State's Attorney that I did not, and would not, commit such a crime. The child's mother also believed us and also went to the State to get the charges dropped. This girl had accused someone else of the same thing.

The State's Attorney told them that it was not in the alleged victim's hands anymore. The State's Attorney told the girl's mother that if she did not continue with the charges, she would be charged with perjury.

For the next 14 months, I waited in jail for my trial as the State tried to build a case that they never had. This was my first time in jail, and it seemed like a lifetime. At the trial, my lawyer talked to the judge and was told that if I was found guilty by a jury I could receive at least 20 years. If I entered a plea bargain, I could get 10 years, and would only have to serve four years and nine months if I got good time. My lawyer advised me to take the 10 years. I had already served nearly half of that time in jail waiting for the trial. This was probably the State's strategy to gain a conviction. I took my lawyer's advice.

After my conviction, I told myself that I could not go on living with an "X" on my head for a crime I did not commit. It was too much for me to handle; therefore, I tried to take my own life. On the night before I was to be transferred to the state penitentiary, I made a rope and hung myself. With the work of God, my life was spared.

[Editor's note: Mr. Blackburn narrowly escaped death in his suicide attempt. He was found hanging in the shower of his dorm room by a fellow inmate who had awakened to use the toilet. He was in complete cardiopulmonary arrest. Paramedics performed CPR en route to the hospital, and he spent the next week on a ventilator in the intensive care unit. Remarkably, he had a full recovery. A suicide note was found at his bedside.]

Being incarcerated, a person endures many hardships and a lot of pain. You have to live with the fact that you cannot go to bed and wake up the next day to be with your loved ones. You have to live your life being told what to do and what not to do. You have to be told when you can go to eat, go to the gym, or go to the yard. You are even told when you can go to church. Tell me what man or woman would want this type of life. How can they expect you to do better when they keep holding you down?

While I was incarcerated, I went through many trials and tribulations. I overcame these by trusting in the Lord. During my stay in prison, I had three surgeries on my leg for a torn Achilles' tendon. There were times when I would be in severe pain, but I was not allowed to take any medicine when I needed it because they only bring the medicine to you at certain times. When I requested medical care, I had to wait three or four days to see a doctor.

I served my four years and nine months with the Illinois Department of Corrections. During this time, I had a clean record. Before I was classified into a minimum prison, they had me with gang-bangers, murderers, armed robbers, and other high level offenders, but I didn't let them bother me. I followed the rules and never made any trouble. I did what I was told to do and what not to do. During the whole time, no one from the prison ever talked to me about the crime that they accused me of.

During the years that I was in prison, several laws changed. Megan's Law came into effect, so now my name must be reported everywhere I live because I was accused of a sex crime. Also, Illinois made a new law so I must be under house arrest until my parole is complete.

I did not know anything about house arrest until I was about to be released from prison. I thought that I would be going home free. I still cannot understand why I am placed under house arrest. I am allowed to leave every day from 6:30 a.m. until 8:00 p.m. to go to work. On the weekends, I can leave from 10:00 a.m. until 10:00 p.m. During this time, if I wanted to hurt someone, I could, so what is the purpose of having me on house arrest? I think house arrest is a big joke, and another way to land a person back in jail. If I am late coming home a few times, I will be sent back.

I am required to wear a locked monitoring bracelet on my leg at all times. As soon as I come within 100 feet of my house, it connects to the telephone. This makes a big inconvenience for my family because the phone makes dialing noises, clicks, and beeps, and interrupts conversations that they are on. The bracelet broke four times, and each time I had to call them and wait for them to come and fix it.

Since I was accused of a sex crime, I am supposed to go to a sex therapy class upon my release. It has been six months since my release and still no one has required me to attend any such class. I haven't heard anything about it. Yet, I am still considered to be a threat.

Now I have to live my life every day wondering when this will end. My parole agent told me that I would be on house arrest for at least a year, but that she could also recommend for me to get out of it in seven months if I follow the rules. I have followed all of the rules without any violations, but now they told me that I will be on house arrest until the year 2000. I went to a hearing, but the lawyer was on vacation so they have to reschedule it.

A few months ago, a detective called on the telephone. He said there was a rape in my town. Even though the computer from my electronic bracelet verified that I was in my house during the time of the rape, they forced me to go to the police line-up. The woman said I was not the person.

All of this should bring me down. But I will not let that happen because I have a friend, and his name is Jesus.

26

A Lesson From Another Country

Kim Marie Thorburn

Deprivation of freedom is a universal form of punishment. In countries around the world, however, the methods of achieving this vary widely. During my inspections of prison systems throughout the world, I have been moved to wonder, is the experience inherently brutal or is an abusive prison system a reflection of the society from which it arises? The prisons of a country are often the most revealing threads of its fabric.

In this chapter, I discuss the South African prison system, one of several foreign prisons where I have done extensive investigations. Its relevance to the United States comes from the shared histories of racial segregation, capitalistic economies, high fear of crime, and zealous imprisonment. The dangers within the South African system should promote our introspection in the United States.

Leaving Apartheid Behind

In 1994, the world watched breathlessly when South Africans ushered in the post-apartheid era by electing their most famous anti-apartheid leader, Nelson Mandela, as president. It was a bloodless revolution, almost incredible considering the years of bloody oppression suffered by the black African majority. Apartheid dismantled, the country sought to instill a culture of human rights to replace the vestiges of the brutal dehumanizing racism that had perpetuated the power of a white minority. The post-apartheid constitution enshrined the values of the Universal Declaration of Human Rights. A quasi-governmental Human Rights Commission was created to receive and resolve citizens' complaints about human rights violations and to report to the president. Disclosure and contrition were used as means to heal.

A laborious process was undertaken to develop a new correctional services act that would define the rights of prisoners in the context of the constitution, provide them with a committee of visitors with whom they could air their grievances, and protect them from abuses through regular monitoring by a judicial inspectorate. Many of the first generation of post-apartheid leaders had themselves been confined, and their proposed legislation would be one of the world's most advanced blueprints for ensuring the protection of prisoners' rights.

South African Prison Reform: The Reality

The reality in South African prisons, however, is still a stark contrast to the prison reform legislation. Fear of crime in South Africa has been intense, and since the fall of apartheid South Africans have witnessed a rise of serious crimes. Upscale residential neighborhoods in urban areas resemble fortressed enclaves, and episodes of random violence and robbery are rife throughout the country. Given this environment, few rally to the cause of prisoners' rights.

South Africa has several hundred jails and prisons administered by a centralized agency, the Department of Correctional Services, but day-to-day activities are conducted by strong, independent, provincial directorates. The facilities house a diverse population, including individuals awaiting sentencing, those already sentenced, juveniles, men, and women. Overcrowding is endemic, a daily average of 110,000 individuals housed in a space designed for roughly 88,000. Naturally, this compromises security. Escapes are rampant, estimated at more than 95 per month. Violence is a common occurrence and often attributed to long-standing prison gang rivalries. These day-to-day realities divert attention from any prison administration attempting to introduce fundamental reform focusing on prisoners' rights.

The challenge is further compounded by residuals of apartheid, deeply ingrained in the system. Guard brutality remains a systemic problem. The prison culture has not evolved from its apartheid-era paramilitary philosophy and organization. This resistance to change was blamed for several excessively violent inmate-staff incidents.

Pollsmoor Prison

In May 1997, I toured Pollsmoor Prison outside of Cape Town. The alarm siren sounded during my inspection. Two prisoners had escaped after holding a guard hostage for a short period. Reportedly, the prisoners had a gun.

The prison closed down while all staff responded, conducting a search for the weapon on the unit that had housed the escapees. A SWAT team took positions on the surrounding rooftops, aiming high-powered rifles into the grounds. The prisoners, nearly all of whom were black, were herded off the unit and crammed into trucks. To reach the trucks, the prisoners had to run through a line of white guards holding attack dogs on leashes. To the amusement of the handlers, the dogs were allowed to lunge and snap at the frightened prisoners just out of reach. Once all of the prisoners were loaded into trucks, a team of guards assembled to search the unit. This team was also composed entirely of white staff. Even though the staff included both black and white guards, I observed several black guards refusing to become involved in any action.

The search turned up a rope made from sheets, but no weapons. Once the search was completed, the prisoners were allowed to return to their unit, but not before passing through the gauntlet of guards and dogs once again.

Less than a week after this incident, another team was brought into Pollsmoor Prison to search for weapons. The team was a special emergency response unit composed of specialists from other prisons throughout the Western Cape Province. The Pollsmoor and provincial correctional administrations were acting on information that corrupt Pollsmoor staff were involved in weapons smuggling.

The task unit, composed of a majority of white guards, entered Pollsmoor early one morning and took the facilities over for approximately eight hours. Most reports concerning the unit's operation pointed to unleashed mayhem, including the beating of many prisoners with pistols and batons and the theft of prisoner property. Hundreds of prisoners were injured, including eight who were hospitalized. Prisoners also complained about racial slurs and other verbal abuse. The search turned up a few prison-made knives but no guns. Dangerous items were reportedly left behind by the task unit, fueling speculation about the intention of their actions.

Vestiges of Violence

My observation of the first incident and the reports of the second signaled that the seething racism of the apartheid era continues at Pollsmoor Prison. The legacy also overflows into staff relations, where tensions among several correctional labor unions take on racist overtones and sometimes result in violent eruptions.

Observers and monitors attribute the continuation of guard brutality to inadequate training and lack of disciplinary consequences. Solutions to bring about change, however, are not that simple. Generations of institutionalized brutality have left an imprint on both former oppressors and the oppressed too deep to easily achieve respect for human dignity and bring an end to violence. Even as the open society strived to heal its wounds and ally itself with human rights and equality, prison risks remained an echo of the past.

Another contradiction between the official prison reform movement and the reality of post-apartheid South African prisons is the introduction of American-style "supermax" prisons. Cloaked in a promise of improved security, such facilities further institutionalize punishment. These facilities are contrary to the values of the South African constitution and are, by their very nature, brutal and abusive. This polarity between words and actions seems to be another residual of apartheid.

Implications

A violent society predictably evokes brutal sanctions. Individual dignity is dismissed by dehumanizing adversaries. As long as such dehumanization exists, the risk for violence continues. Violence will persist in prisons, because their nature is antagonistic to human dignity even as the open society attempts to heal.

The lesson for the United States is to ensure that human dignity is a universal franchise—one that extends beyond the free society.

27

Death Penalty
The Ultimate Violence

Steven S. Spencer

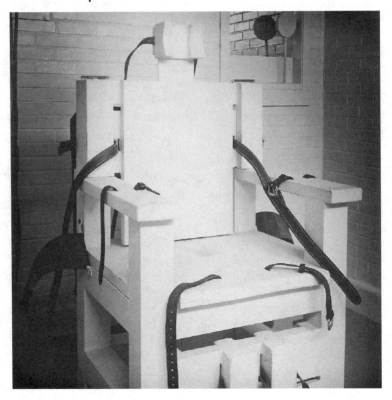

Figure 27.1 The electric chair in Oklahoma.

Photograph by Toshi Kazama. Reprinted with permission.

*To those who suggested that the god of freedom might be achieved more ex-
pediently by violent means, Gandhi replied, "Your reasoning is the same as
saying that we can get a rose through planting a noxious weed. . . I am more
concerned with preventing the brutalization of human nature than with the
prevention of the sufferings of my own people."*

R. Schneinin, *The New Mexican*, p. F-2.

In the 1970s I was a member of the medical faculty of the University of Arizona,
and responded to a request for consultation and teaching at the Arizona State
Prison. My orientation tour included a visit to the death house. The death house
was a small building standing separate from the others. It contained two cells
where condemned inmates would spend their last days, a gas chamber, and an
observation area around the chamber. There was a red phone that had a direct
connection to the governor's office, representing the last glimmer of hope for a
last-minute reprieve. Around the gas chamber was a photo gallery, with pictures
of all of those executed by the state of Arizona. For those executed in earlier days
by hanging, the noose was also there, tacked to the wall next to the photographs.

It was a macabre scene, and my escort, a young surgeon, told me a grisly tale
about one of the pictures. It was that of a woman, obviously obese, who was executed at the old territorial prison in Yuma, by hanging. When she was dropped
through the trap door, the noose held, but her neck did not. Her head came off,
blood spurted all over the spectators, and the governor threw up. That was the
last execution by hanging in Arizona, I was told.

It may also have been the last time an Arizona governor attended an execution, which is lamentable. Governors should attend all of the executions they
sanction. Prosecuting attorneys and judges who call for the death penalty should
also attend all of their execution events. They should be required by law to witness the outcome of their action or inaction. Of course, such a law is not likely to
be passed, because it would threaten the stability of the present depersonalized,
unemotional, and remote process of decision making about state killing.

In most states, our society has graduated from hanging and the firing squad to
more refined methods of killing. This has usually been done in the name of a
more merciful and less painful death. The only states that still have hanging or
firing squad as an option also have the gas chamber, electrocution, or lethal injection as a choice ("Breach of Trust," 1994). Lethal injection is the latest development in distancing those responsible for performing the act of killing. Medi-
cally trained personnel insert a needle in a vein. Then the condemned person is
wheeled into the execution chamber on a litter covered with a white sheet, all

very sanitary and hospital-like. The intravenous line is then connected to a lethal injection machine, operated by technicians hidden behind a curtain, where the audience cannot see and identify them. At the signal, the machine is activated, and the criminal is put to death.

This medicalization of the death penalty has greatly disturbed the medical profession. Physicians are trained and indoctrinated to nurture and preserve life. The perversion of medical training and skills to become instruments of death is anathema. In 1980 the American Medical Association adopted a statement that, regardless of an individual's opinion on capital punishment, a physician should not participate in an execution. In 1992 the statement was revised and expanded, to include a detailed explanation of what constitutes participation, including acts of preparing the condemned person for execution, ordering the drugs that are used, giving technical advice, attending an execution as a physician, and monitoring vital signs and pronouncing death (Council on Ethical and Judicial Affairs, 1994). This ethical stand has been endorsed by all medical organizations that have taken a position on the subject, including the American College of Physicians, the American Public Health Association, the American Nurses Association, and a number of state medical societies ("Breach of Trust," 1994).

Unfortunately, the laws of many death penalty states require that a physician be present at executions. When the law requires the performance of acts contrary to professional ethics, the law must be changed. Physicians have been successful in getting the law changed in at least two states, Arizona and Utah, so that they are no longer required to attend executions. However, even if all states were to change their laws in this way, and even if physicians were formally disciplined by their licensing boards for taking part in executions, the death penalty would still be applied. Nonmedical technicians can be trained to place a needle in a vein and become executioners. That certainly requires less skill and practice than swinging the beheading ax in Saudi Arabia. Not until more and more thoughtful voting citizens are repulsed by the taking of a human life in the name of justice, will the death penalty be abolished.

When I became medical director of the New Mexico Corrections Department in 1985, one of the first actions I took was to make sure, as a matter of policy, that no health services personnel would participate in executions in any way. Furthermore, no health services facilities, space, equipment, or drugs would be used. My staff was unanimously greatly relieved to have this policy to guarantee that their relationships with their inmate patients would remain therapeutic and helping.

The New Mexico legislature has gone along with so many other states, in substituting lethal injection for the gas chamber, but in fact New Mexico has not executed anyone since 1960. The death penalty is far less popular with juries than with politicians and prosecutors. There have been approximately 150 capital cases in New Mexico in recent years. About half of these cases have been ably defended by a dedicated public defender team, and only four men are now on death row. The rest have been defended by a private attorney, Gary Mitchell, whose diligent efforts and passion have kept all of those clients from receiving the death sentence (personal communication).

New Mexico is largely a Catholic state, and the Church has taken a stand against the death penalty. In September 1995, the New Mexico Catholic Conference and the three bishops of New Mexico reaffirmed their opposition to capital punishment, citing the 1991 statement of the United States bishops (Sheehan, Pelotte, & Ramirez, 1995):

> In view of our commitment to the value and dignity of human life, we oppose the use of capital punishment. We believe that a return to the use of the death penalty is leading to, indeed can only lead to, further erosion of respect for life in our society. We do not question society's right to punish the offender, but we believe that there are better approaches to protecting our people from violent crimes than resorting to executions. In its application, the death penalty has been discriminatory toward the poor, the indigent, and racial minorities. Our society should reject the death penalty. . . .

Other religious groups have also taken stands against the death penalty. Members of the Religious Society of Friends (Quakers), who believe in the presence of God in each and every person, have long opposed the death penalty. Other religious groups calling for abolition of the death penalty have included the American Baptist Churches in the U.S.A., the American Friends Service Committee, the American Jewish Committee, the Christian Church (Disciples of Christ), Church of the Brethren, Church Women United, The Episcopal Church, the General Conference Mennonite Church, the Mennonite Central Committee U.S., The Mennonite Church, the Lutheran Church in America, The Moravian Church, the National Board YWCA of the U.S.A., the National Council of Churches of Christ in the U.S.A., The Orthodox Church in America, and the Presbyterian Church (U.S.A.) ("The Death Penalty," 1988).

Toney Anaya was governor of New Mexico when I moved there. He had been attorney general before becoming governor. Just before leaving office in 1987, Governor Anaya commuted the sentences of all five men on death row to life imprisonment. It certainly was a controversial act, and reaped more criticism than praise, but Toney Anaya is a man of conscience, and could not leave undone something that he knew was morally necessary for him.

After Anaya, death row began to be occupied again. At the Penitentiary of New Mexico, however, there was no longer a place to do the deed. The gas chamber stood in a basement room that had been used for laundry and uniform supply for years. There were no policies and procedures in place for execution by lethal injection. Reluctance seemed to be pervasive. Corrections officials who have had the responsibility of carrying out executions are far from enthusiastic about it (Martin, 1993; Thigpen, 1993; Vasquez, 1993). Finally the warden was told he had to make preparations. He asked me to give him some advice. He was my friend and colleague. I told him I just couldn't give him any advice, or help in any way, because that would violate my professional ethics as well as my personal convictions. He accepted that graciously, although wardens in some other states have taken or threatened punitive action against medical staff who refused to pervert their training for the purposes of the death penalty ("Breach of Trust," 1994). I left the New Mexico Corrections Department in 1993. Since then the penitentiary in Santa Fe has constructed its death house, but has not yet used it.

Many scholarly studies have shown that the death penalty fails as a deterrent (Bedau, 1997). In states without the death penalty, and in cities in those states, there is less murder and violence than in states with the death penalty (U.S. Bureau of Justice Statistics, 1995). Manhattan District Attorney Robert M. Morgenthau said, before New York recently adopted the death penalty, "Take it from someone who has spent a career in Federal and state law enforcement, enacting the death penalty . . . would be a grave mistake. Prosecutors must reveal the dirty little secret they too often share only among themselves: The death penalty actually hinders the fight against crime" ("On the Front Line," 1995, p. 1). Willie L. Williams, Los Angeles chief of Police, said, "I am not convinced that capital punishment, in and of itself, is a deterrent to crime because most people do not think about the death penalty before they commit a violent or capital crime" ("On the Front Line," 1995, p. 1).

Attorney General Janet Reno has said, "I think that the only purpose for the death penalty, as I see it, is vengeance—pure and simple vengeance. But I think vengeance is a very personal feeling and I don't think it is something that civilized government should engage in. . ." ("On the Front Line," 1995, p. 1). Her opinion is shared by many experienced law enforcement authorities. A 1995 poll of 388 police chiefs and sheriffs found that they ranked the death penalty last as a way of reducing violent crime, and rated it as the least cost-effective method for controlling crime. Most of them did not believe that the death penalty is a significant deterrent, because murderers do not consider the range of possible punishments. These law enforcement officers thought that political debates about the death penalty distract legislators from focusing on real solutions to crime (Murphy, 1995).

The death penalty has also been shown to have killed many innocent people (Roos, 1997). A Stanford Law Review study found that, in this century, there were 350 capital convictions in which the defendants were subsequently found to be not guilty. Of those wrongly convicted, 25 were executed (Bedau & Radelet, 1987). As columnist Jim Belshaw of the Albuquerque Journal wrote, "If you support the death penalty, and you're being honest with yourself, you have a math problem to solve: How many innocent people are you willing to execute?

(If executing innocent people doesn't bother you, you have more than a math problem)" (Belshaw, 1998).

Twelve of our United States have abolished the death penalty. The argument has often been presented to the Supreme Court that the death penalty is cruel and unusual punishment, and therefore a violation of the Eighth Amendment to our constitution. Supreme Court Justice Harry Blackmun, in a dissenting opinion in 1994, said, "From this day forward, I no longer shall tinker with the machinery of death. . . I feel morally and intellectually obligated to concede that the death penalty experiment has failed" (*Callins v. James,* 1994).

In the current political "get tough on crime" atmosphere, our society has had to face some death penalty issues about which there is notable ambivalence, to say the least. As legislatures try to lower the eligibility age for execution, how willing are we to kill children? There seems to be a reluctance to execute the mentally retarded, but not the mentally ill, unless the mentally ill criminal is insane by legal definition. But the mentally ill person has to be mentally competent at the time of execution, so that he or she can understand the significance of the punishment. If not competent, he or she should be treated until competence is achieved. And there is much more reluctance to execute a woman than a man. What a tangled web we weave! If you commit a capital crime in our country, an execution outcome depends on whether you are a man or a woman, in what state you are tried, on the age that state considers eligible for execution, on your race, on the race of your victim, on your economic status, on how good a defense attorney you have, and on whether you are mentally ill or mentally retarded.

These inequities are responsible for the increasing popularity of life in prison without parole as an alternative to the death penalty. When Americans have been polled on this, support for the death penalty drops considerably when the option of life without parole is presented as an alternative ("Sentencing for Life," 1993). In February 1998 the state of Texas executed Karla Faye Tucker, a woman who by all accounts was not the same personality as she was at the time of her brutal crime 14 years earlier. The fact that she had turned her life around did not spare her from execution, but did lead many people to have second thoughts about capital punishment. After her execution, a poll in Texas showed a drop of 17% in support for the death penalty (Ayres, 1998).

Ours is the only Western industrialized nation with the death penalty. The enthusiasm to execute criminals in this country has created some problems with our international relations. In April 1998, Arizona executed a Honduran and Virginia executed a Paraguayan, causing demonstrations and a straining of relations with those two countries. A State Department official acknowledged that both cases were tainted by violations of the defendants' rights under the Vienna Convention, which requires that people arrested in a foreign country be advised of their right to contact officials of their own country within a short time. Earlier in the year, Texas had executed two Mexicans, fraying our relations with that country, which, like many Latin American countries, has no death penalty (Stout, 1998).

What is it about us as people, as enlightened human beings, that makes us want to take a life in punishment for taking a life? Clarence Darrow put it this way in 1924 ("Clarence Darrow on the Death Penalty," 1991):

> In the end, this question is simply one of the humane feelings against the brutal feelings. One who likes to see suffering, out of what he thinks is a righteous indignation, or any other, will hold fast to capital punishment. One who has sympathy, imagination, kindness and understanding, will hate it and detest it as he hates and detests death. (p. 62)

The death penalty cannot be applied equitably or infallibly, and denies both the sacredness of human life and the capacity for people to change. We live in a violent society. It is essential that we make an effort to counter the political oratory that insults our intelligence with its simplistic approaches to violence, and that cries for the execution of more criminals. The death penalty only reinforces a primitive lust for vengeance. Because it is done in our name, it does violence to each and every one of us, and thereby contributes to the culture of violence in this country. In our criminal justice system the death penalty is the ultimate violence.

References

Ayres, B. D., Jr. (1998, March 23). Death penalty support declines after execution. *The New York Times.*

Bedau, H. A. (1997). Capital punishment is not a deterrent to capital crimes. *The case against the death penalty.* American Civil Liberties Union. ttp://www.aclu.org/library/case_against_death.html (Available on the World Wide Web, June 6, 1999.)

Bedau, H., & Radelet, M. (1987). Miscarriages of justice in potentially capital cases. *Stanford Law Review, 40,* 21-179.

Belshaw, J. (1998, April 10). Life and death math problem. *Albuquerque Journal.*

Breach of trust: Physician participation in executions in the United States. (1994). Report. Available from any of the publishing organizations: Philadelphia: The American College of Physicians; New York: Human Rights Watch; Washington, DC: National Coalition to Abolish the Death Penalty; Boston: Physicians for Human Rights.

Callins v. James. U.S. Supreme Court on Writ of Certiorari to the United States Court of Appeals for the Fifth Circuit. No. 93-7054. Decided Feb. 22, 1994.

Clarence Darrow on the death penalty. (1991). Evanston, IL: Chicago Historical Bookworks.

Council on Ethical and Judicial Affairs. (1994). *Code of medical ethics, current opinions with annotations.* Chicago: American Medical Association.

Martin, G. N., III. (1993, July). Enforcing the death penalty with competence, compassion. *Corrections Today,* 60-64.

Murphy, P. V. (1995, February 23). Death penalty useless. *USA Today.*

On the front line: Law enforcement views on the death penalty. (1995, February). Report. Washington, DC: The Death Penalty Information Center.

Roos, S. J. (1997, November 13). *Death penalty's lessons.* The Christian Science Monitor.

Schneinin, R. (1998, February 7). Nonviolence. *The New Mexican,* p. F-2. Santa Fe, NM.

Sentencing for life: Americans embrace alternatives to the death penalty. (1993, April). Report. Washington, DC: The Death Penalty Information Center.

Sheehan, Most Rev. M. J., Pelotte, Most Rev. D. E., & Ramirez, Most Rev. R. (1995, September 19). *New Mexico Catholic Conference opposes death penalty.* [Press release]. Albuquerque: New Mexico Catholic Bishops.

Stout, D. (1998, April 26). U.S. executions draw scorn from abroad. *The New York Times,* Week in Review, p. 4.

The death penalty: The religious community calls for abolition. (1988). Washington, DC: National Coalition to Abolish the Death Penalty.

Thigpen, M. L. (1993, July). A tough assignment. *Corrections Today,* 57-58.

U.S. Bureau of Justice Statistics. (1995). Murder and non-negligent manslaughter in states with and without the death penalty. *Source book of criminal justice statistics 1995.* Washington, DC: Government Printing Office.

Vasquez, D. B. (1993, July). Helping prison staff handle the stress of an execution. *Corrections Today,* 70-72.

Postscript

John P. May

While the chapters for this book were being written and collected, I would occasionally mention the project to different people. Those who were not familiar with corrections were somewhat skeptical of the hypothesis that prison growth could be contributing to violence in our society. After they considered it, however, they were always quick to ask what the alternative would be.

On the other hand, those who worked in jails or prisons needed no explanation. They were quick to agree that the system causes harm. In fact, it was disturbing that nearly every experienced person believed the system to be detrimental. And they didn't ask me what the alternative would be. I think they know the answer. They realize that the answer is not putting people into the system in the first place. Once they are there, failure is too common. As penal reformer Jerry Miller once said, "The best service you can do for anyone who finds himself caught up in the criminal justice system is to get him out of it as quickly as possible."[1] Reducing the number of prison admissions can be accomplished in many ways, including reexamination of the many mandatory sentencing laws that remove discretion from the judicial system, developing alternative community restitution or treatment programs, and investing in prevention strategies to reduce the temptation or opportunity to make bad choices or mistakes.

There will always be evildoers and predators, and prison might be the best response for them. The tremendous jump in this country's incarceration curve, however, was not caused by an increase in the numbers of such persons, but rather by deliberate policy changes that incarcerate the nonviolent with the violent, the one-mistake young person with the career criminal. The antitherapeutic and harsh environment of prison is not the place for these individuals. The harm of this practice is becoming apparent: We are propagating violence throughout our communities.

Note

1. Snell, M. B. (1995, Sept.-Oct.). Habitat for inhumanity. *Utne Reader,* pp. 82-91; quote on p. 88. (Interview adapted with permission from *The Humanist,* Jan/Feb 1994).

Index

About the Contributors

Elizabeth Alexander is Director of the National Prison Project of the American Civil Liberties Union Foundation. Prior to her appointment as Director in 1996, she was the Project's Associate Director for Litigation. She is one of the county's foremost experts on prison conditions litigation, and has argued numerous prisoners' rights cases in federal trial and appellate courts, including *Farmer v. Brennan, Wilson v. Seiter,* and *Lewis v. Casey* in the Supreme Court of the United States. She is a graduate of Yale Law School and Brandeis University. Before joining the National Prison Project in 1981, she worked in Wisconsin as an assistant state public defender in the Madison Appellate Office and was also a staff attorney with the Madison Corrections Legal Services Program. She was the first Visitor from Practice at the University of Southern California Law Center.

B. Jaye Anno, PhD, CCHP-A, is a criminologist specializing in correctional health administration and compliance with national correctional health care standards. She currently operates a consulting firm with her partner, Bernard P. Harrison, with whom she also founded the National Commission on Correctional Health Care (NCCHC) in 1983. She is an experienced researcher, lecturer, and author in correctional health care. She is the principal author of the major reference book for the field, *Prison Health Care: Guidelines For the Management of an Adequate Delivery System,* and has written numerous other articles on correctional health care topics. She is also the editor of the *Journal of Correctional Health Care.* She has been the recipient of the Distinguished Service Award of the American Correctional Health Services Association as well as the NCCHC's Award of Merit.

Randy Blackburn grew up in Batesville, Mississippi. He came to Illinois in 1989 in search of new employment opportunities. He worked as a truck driver there until he was incarcerated, and upon release was rehired by the same company. He has one son.

Alfred Blumstein, PhD is a university professor and the J. Erik Jonsson Professor of Operations Research and former Dean of the H. John Heinz III School of Public Policy and Management of Carnegie Mellon University. He is Director of the National Consortium on Violence Research (NCOVR), a long-term project funded by the National Science Foundation. He has chaired NAS panels on deterrence and incapacitation, sentencing, and criminal careers. He served as chairman of the Pennsylvania Commission on Crime and Delinquency (1979-1990), the state criminal justice planning agency, and was a member of the state's Sentencing Commission (1986-1996). He has received the American Society of Criminology's Sutherland Award for "contributions to research," and was president of the Society (1991-1992). He has been awarded the honorary degree of Doctor of Laws by the John Jay College of Criminal Justice. His research related to crime and punishment has covered issues of criminal careers, deterrence and incapacitation, sentencing, incarceration practice and policy, racial disproportionality, youth violence, and demographic trends. He was elected to the National Academy of Engineering in 1998.

Shawn D. Bushway, PhD is currently a postdoctoral Fellow for the National Consortium on Violence Research working at the University of Maryland, Department of Criminology and Criminal Justice, under the direction of Dr. Raymond Paternoster. He received his PhD in Public Policy Analysis and Political Economy in 1996 from the H. John Heinz III School of Public Policy and Management at Carnegie Mellon University. His dissertation, entitled "The impact of a criminal record on access to legitimate employment," formed the basis for the chapter included in this book. He is also the coauthor, with Dr. Peter Reuter, of a chapter in a report for the U.S. Congress titled "Preventing Crime: What Works, What Doesn't, What's Promising," which reviews evaluations of employment programs aimed at preventing crime. His current research focuses on understanding the role of employment in leading to desistance from crime.

Fernando Chang-Muy is Adjunct Professor at the University of Pennsylvania School of Law, teaching Immigration and Refugee Law, and at Swarthmore College teaching International Human Rights. He is a former legal officer with the Office of the United Nations High Commissioner for Refugees and with the World Health Organization, and is currently Program Officer at The Philadelphia Foundation, coordinating a funding initiative which provides financial support to nonprofit agencies that work with immigrants and refugees.

Robert L. Cohen is a physician in private practice in New York City. A graduate of Rush Medical College, he first worked with prisoners at the Cook County Jail in Chicago in 1975. In 1979 he began working with colleagues at Cook County Hospital and Northwestern University, investigating the relationship between violence and epilepsy. He served as the director of the Montefiore Rikers Island Health Services (1981 to 1986), and subsequently spent two years as the 14th vice president for Medical Operations for the New York City Health and Hospitals Corporation. He has been a court-appointed monitor responsible for overseeing medical care for prisoners in correctional systems in Florida, Washington, D.C., Philadelphia, Connecticut, and New York state. He is the representative of the American Public Health Association on the National Commission for Correctional Health Care. In New York City, he serves on the Boards of the Fortune Society and the Housing Works Day Treatment Centers.

Bernardine Dohrn is Director of the Children and Family Justice Center at the Legal Clinic of Northwestern University School of Law. She is a graduate of both the University of Chicago College and the Law School. Her publications include: "Violence By and Against Youngsters at the Millennium" in *Children in Trouble With the Law,* forthcoming (Margaret Rosenheim and Mark Testa, Eds.); "We Die Soon: Children, Violence and the Law" in the *Maryland Journal of Contemporary Legal Issues*; "Bad Mothers, Good Mothers, and the State: Children On the Margins" in *The University of Chicago Law School Roundtable;* and "Youth Violence: False Fears and Hard Truths" in *Educational Leadership.* She is a founding member of the American Bar Association (ABA) Steering Committee on the Unmet Legal Needs of Children, and a member and founding cochair of the ABA Section of Litigation's Task Force on Children.

Stephen J. Ingley, is Executive Director of the American Jail Association (AJA). He is a member of the U.S. Department of Justice's Corrections Technology Advisory Council and is commissioner for the International Association of Correctional Officers' Commission on Correctional Curriculum in Higher Education. He publishes regularly on corrections-related issues, makes numerous public appearances as a panelist and keynote speaker, and was the recipient of the first annual Jail Industries Association Founders Award. He holds a bachelor's degree in government and politics from the University of Maryland.

Joanne Mariner is Associate Counsel at Human Rights Watch, an international human rights organization based in New York. Her work involves monitoring human right abuses against prisoners around the world, and she has written or cowritten the following reports: *Cold Storage: Super-Maximum Security Con-*

finement in Indiana; Prison Conditions in Hong Kong in 1997; All Too Familiar: Sexual Abuse of Women Prisoners In U.S. State Prisons; and *Punishment Before Trial: Prison Conditions in Venezuela.* She received a law degree from Yale Law School in 1992, and served for a year as judicial clerk to the Honorable Stephen Reinhardt, a federal judge on the Court of Appeals for the Ninth Circuit.

Steve J. Martin, BS, MA is in private practice as a corrections consultant and is actively involved in prison litigation in various states, including California, New York, Ohio, Maryland, Montana, and Utah. He is involved in jail litigation in cities that include New York City, Pittsburgh, and Milwaukee, and serves as expert to the U.S. Department of Justice, Civil Rights Division, in both prison and jail cases in South Carolina, Mississippi, and Nevada. He has worked as a consultant in more than 20 states and has visited or inspected more than 500 confinement facilities in the United States. He received his BS and MA in Correctional Administration from Sam Houston State University and his JD from the University of Tulsa. During more than 25 years in the criminal justice field, he has worked as a prison guard, a probation and parole officer, and a prosecutor. He is the former general counsel for the Texas prison system, and served gubernatorial appointments in Texas on both a sentencing commission and a council for mentally impaired offenders. He coauthored a book on Texas prisons and has written numerous articles on criminal justice issues. He has served as an adjunct faculty member at six different universities, including the University of Texas School of Law.

Marc Mauer, MA has served as Assistant Director of The Sentencing Project in Washington, D.C., since 1987. He is the author of some of the most widely cited publications in the field of criminal justice, including *Young Black Men and the Criminal Justice System, Americans Behind Bars,* a series comparing international rates of incarceration, and *Race to Incarcerate.* He is the recipient of the Helen Buttenweiser Award from the Fortune Society and the Donald Cressey Award for contributions to criminal justice research from the National Council on Crime and Delinquency. He holds a Master of Social Work degree from the University of Michigan.

John P. May, MD, FACP, is the Midwest Regional Medical Director for Prison Health Services, overseeing medical care for prisoners in the State of Indiana and other regions. He has been a senior physician at the Cook County Department of Corrections in Chicago and assistant medical director for the Central Detention Facility in Washington, D.C. He is a consultant for the U.S. Department of Justice Civil Rights Division, investigating jail and prison health services, and a board member of the Society of Correctional Physicians. He completed his residency at Cook County Hospital in 1992 and is board certified in internal medicine. He is a Fellow of the American College of Physicians. In addition to his correctional work, he is recognized for his research and leadership in violence prevention initiatives. He is a board member of Operation Clean Break, a gang tattoo removal program in Chicago, the Handgun Epidemic Lowering Plan (HELP) Network, and others. He is a member of the Homicide Research Working Group and editorial board member of the *Journal of Homicide Studies*. He received the 1995 Public Service Award of the Illinois State Medical Society, and the American College of Physicians' 1996 Rosenthal Foundation Award for original approach and effectiveness in the delivery of health care.

Kenneth L. McGinnis is Senior Vice-President of Security Response Technologies, Middleton, MA and Lansing, MI. His correctional career includes 26 years as a corrections professional with the Illinois and Michigan Departments of Corrections. He served as the director of the Michigan Department of Corrections from March 1991 to January 1999, and was director of the Illinois Department of Corrections and a warden at three different Illinois prisons.

Colleen R. McLaughlin, PhD is Assistant Professor in the Departments of Surgery and Emergency Medicine at the Medical College of Virginia, Virginia Commonwealth University. She earned her doctorate in psychology from Dartmouth College, and completed a five-year postdoctoral fellowship in the Department of Pharmacology and Toxicology at the Medical College of Virginia. She has organized an ongoing collaborative effort between criminal justice and health care professionals within the Commonwealth of Virginia. Her current research involves epidemiological, prevention, and treatment research on the relationship between substance use, drug selling, criminal offending, and lethal and nonlethal violence. The specific aims of this ongoing research program are to identify and characterize violent events, in an effort to enhance investigative efficacy as well as community-based prevention. She is particularly interested in the identification of potential interactive variables operating between the victim and perpetrator, which may yield critical risk factors and situational variables relating to the escalation of a behavioral interaction or dispute into a homicidal event.

JoAnne Page is Executive Director of The Fortune Society, one of the oldest and most established ex-offender self-help advocacy and service organizations in the country, a position she has held since March 1989. She graduated from Yale Law School with a Juris Doctor degree in 1980 and worked through 1983 in Brooklyn as a criminal defense attorney with the Legal Aid Society. From 1983 to 1986 she developed and managed programs that provided alternatives to incarceration for felony defendants at the Court Employment Project in New York City. Her experience in criminal justice dates back to 1972, when she began teaching and counseling in New York State prisons. She heads the Executive Committee of the Board of Trustees of the Milton S. Eisenhower Foundation and served as a commissioner on the National Criminal Justice Commission. She speaks nationally on criminal justice issues and makes frequent television appearances in such diverse settings as CNN, Court TV, and a broad range of talk shows.

Roger H. Peters, PhD is Associate Professor in the Department of Mental Health Law and Policy at the University of South Florida, Louis de la Ponte Florida Mental Health Institute, where he has been a faculty member since 1986. He received his PhD in clinical psychology from the Florida State University, following a pre-doctoral internship at the University of North Carolina. He is the lead consultant to the National GAINS Center, a collaborative multi-year project sponsored by CMHS, CSAT, and NIC, designed to improve services for individuals with co-occurring mental health and substance use disorders in the justice system. He has been awarded numerous grants and contracts, and has published widely in areas of substance abuse screening and assessment, relapse prevention, treatment, co-occurring disorders, and program evaluation within the criminal justice system. He currently serves on the Board of Directors for the National Association of Drug Court Professionals.

Khalid R. Pitts, BA, MA is Director of State Programs for the Educational Fund to End Handgun Violence and the Director of State Legislation for the Coalition to Stop Gun Violence. Formerly, he was a health administrator at the Central Detention Facility in Washington, D.C., and continues his work the Facility as a consultant. He helped found and serves as a board member of a *City Without Gun Violence,* a coalition of health care professionals, law enforcement agencies, and community organizations dedicated to prevention of firearm violence. He also serves on the board of directos of *UMRUNTU,* a restorative justice organization working with juvenile offenders and their victims. He has held the position of senior researcher at the National Institutes of Health, where he implemented a research protocol to reduce adolescent pregnancy within the District of Columbia and has worked as a site director for the Harvard School of Public Health, administering a school- and clinically-based violence prevention program. He was the project director for The Beverly Coleman Miller Group, Inc., where he designed and supervised a project to develop services for children in public housing who have witnessed violence, and he was a member of several Mayoral task forces to reduce juvenile violence in Wasington, D.C. He earned his undergraduate degree in history from The College of The Holy Cross and has a Master in Public Health from George Wasington University.

William J. Rold, JD, CCHP is a practicing attorney in New York City with 20 years' experience in corrections. He graduated Phi Beta Kappa from Duke University, and received his law degree from Georgetown University Law Center in 1977. He has practiced law in Washington, D.C., Alaska, Tennessee, and New York, at all levels of state and federal courts. He is certified as a Correctional Health Care Professional–Advanced by the National Commission on Correctional Health Care, where he serves as a Trustee. He is on the editorial board of the *Journal of Correctional Health Care* and a member of the Advisory Board of the Mental Health in Corrections Consortium. He is chair of the Sub-Committee on Standards on Corrections and Sentencing of the American Bar Association and a member of numerous organizations with interest in corrections, including the American Public Health Association, the American Correctional Health Services Association, and the American Correctional Association. He has written and lectured extensively over the last 20 years on issues related to corrections, ethics, standards, and the law, and has consulted with the U.S. Department of Justice, the Academy of Criminal Justice Sciences, the U.S. Department of Health and Human Services, the United States Information Agency, and the Epilepsy Foundation of America, among others.

Miriam A. Rollin, Esq. has been an advocate for at-risk children, youth, and families for the past 17 years. Prior to her current work as the Director of Public Policy for the National Network for Youth, she served for four years as vice president of the National Association of Child Advocates. Her previous policy work included six years as a federal policy advocate on children, youth, and family-related issues, representing the National PTA and other organizations. She is also an attorney, and practiced for five years in child and family-related cases in New York, Maryland, and Washington, D.C., primarily in juvenile delinquency and abuse/neglect proceedings. She has also performed legal research and writing for the American Bar Association's Center on Children and the Law. She has served on the Board of the National Association of Counsel for Children since 1991, and is its recent past president.

Mark Soler is President of the Youth Law Center, a national public interest law firm with offices in San Francisco and Washington, D.C. A 1973 graduate of Yale Law School, for the past 20 years he has provided training, technical assistance, and counsel to public officials, agency administrators and staffs, parents, community groups, attorneys, and other children's advocates in states throughout the country on juvenile justice and related issues, and has litigated successfully in nine states on behalf of children subjected to dangerous conditions of confinement. He has also written more than 20 articles and book chapters on civil rights issues and the rights of children, and has taught at Boston College Law School, the Washington College of Law at American University, Boston

University School of Law, the University of Nebraska Law School, and San Francisco State University. He has received awards for his work from the American Psychological Association, American Bar Association, and Western Society of Criminology, and from the Alliance for Juvenile Justice, which is composed of national organizations of juvenile justice detention and corrections professionals.

Steven S. Spencer, MD is an independent consultant in correctional health care, after serving for eight years as Medical Director for the New Mexico Corrections Department. He has evaluated care in U.S. prisons and jails for various state and local jurisdictions, for the U.S. Justice Department, the National Commission on Correctional Health Care, the National Institute of Corrections, and federal court special masters, and in 1994 evaluated health care in Cambodian prisons. He has also served as an expert witness in litigation cases. His other experience includes heart disease research at Albert Schweitzer's hospital in Gabon, Africa; the practice of internal medicine in Flagstaff, Arizona and on the Navajo Reservation; and nine years in full-time faculty positions at the University of Arizona and the University of Dar es Salaam, Tanzania. He is a board certified internist and a Fellow of the American College of Physicians.

Kim Marie Thorburn, MD, MPH is a human rights activist who has consulted on prison health for Amnesty International and Physicians for Human Rights. She has inspected prison systems in Israel, the West Bank, South Africa, Zimbabwe, Denmark, El Salvador, and many jurisdictions in the United States. Her experience comes from 20 years as a prison physician in California and Hawaii. The author of numerous articles on prison health care, she has written extensively on prisoner injury and the death penalty. She is currently a public health official in Spokane, Washington.

Corey Weinstein, MD serves as Chair of the Corcoran Committee of California Prison Focus (CPF), a human rights and advocacy organization working with and for prisoners in California's control units since 1990. Under his direction, CPF has investigated and protested ongoing human rights violations at California State Prison at Corcoran and its Security Housing Unit. For the past 25 years, he has served as a correctional medical expert for prisoners in class action and individual lawsuits against jails and prisons in California. As chair of the Jail and Prison Health Committee of the American Public Health Association, he coordinated the preparation of *AIDS 1995 Update: For the Standards of Health Services In Correctional Institutions*. He coauthored a landmark study of disciplinary practices in U.S. prisons, "The Myth of Humane Imprisonment: A Critical Analysis of Severe Discipline In Maximum Security Prisons, 1945-1990," published in *Prison Violence In America* in 1994.

Andrea Weisman, PhD is Director of Mental Health Services for the Receiver for Medical and Mental Health Services at the District of Columbia Central Detention Facility, and has been the director of the federally-funded D.C. Women's Jail Project. She received her PhD in clinical psychology from Clark University. She serves as a consultant to the monitor overseeing Georgia's juvenile detention facilities, and has worked for or served as consultant to national correctional mental health advocacy organizations such as the Center on Crime, Communities and Culture of the Open Society Institute; the National Coalition for Mental and Substance Abuse Health Care in the Justice System; the National GAINS Center; the Pelican Bay Information Project; Death Penalty Focus; and the Bazelon Center for Mental Health Law. In the 10 years prior to her involvement in correctional mental health care, she worked in clinical administrative capacities in the public mental health system. Her publications include *Mental Health Outpatient Services In Correctional Settings.*

Tony L. Whitehead, PhD, MS Hyg is Professor of Medical Anthropology, and Director (and founder) of the "Cultural Systems Analysis Group" (CuSAG), Department of Anthropology at the University of Maryland. He received a Masters of Science in Hygiene degree in Public Health in 1969, and a PhD in Anthropology from the University of Pittsburgh in 1976. He was a faculty member in the Department of Health Education, School of Public Health, University of North Carolina, Chapel Hill (1976 to 1987), where he developed research and program development models that integrate anthropological methods and theories and health program applications, particularly in community-based settings. He has broad research and technical assistance experiences in the United States, the Caribbean, Africa, and Europe, related to topics including AIDS, cancer, hypertension, men and family planning, adolescent motherhood, and evaluations of community health and development programs. As a researcher, his expertise is in ethnographic and qualitative methods used in community assessment research and program evaluation. His research has received support from many organizations, including the Russell Sage Foundation, the Agency for International Development, the Centers for Disease Control, the National Heart, Lung and Blood Institute, and the National Cancer Institute. He has published 2 books and over 30 journal articles and book chapters in his areas of research interest.

Juan Williams, one of America's leading political writers and thinkers, is author of *American Revolutionary,* the critically acclaimed biography of Associate Supreme Court Justice Thurgood Marshall. He is also author of the nonfiction best-seller *Eyes On the Prize—America's Civil Rights Years, 1954-1965,* the companion volume to the celebrated PBS television series. He is a political analyst and national correspondent for the *Washington Post,* the Washington Political Analyst for Fox News Channel, and a panelist for Fox News Sunday. He serves as host of "America's Black Forum," a nationally syndicated news show on critical issues affecting black America. He served as substitute co-host on CNN "Crossfire" for many years and was a regular panelist for five years on "Inside Washington." He has won an Emmy Award for TV documentary writing and won widespread critical acclaim for a series of documentaries including "Politics—The New Black Power" and his PBS documentary on A. Philip Randolph. His articles have appeared in *Fortune, The Atlantic Monthly, Ebony,* and *Gentleman's Quarterly.* He has appeared on numerous television programs, including "Nightline," CNN's "Capitol Gang," "Washington Week in Review," "Arsenio," and "Oprah."